MIND SIGHTS

ORIGINAL VISUAL ILLUSIONS,
AMBIGUITIES, AND OTHER ANOMALIES,
WITH A COMMENTARY ON THE
PLAY OF MIND IN
PERCEPTION AND ART

ROGER N. SHEPARD

W. H. FREEMAN AND COMPANY
NEW YORK

Library of Congress Cataloging-in-Publication Data

Shepard, Roger N.
Mind sights : original visual illusions, ambiguities, and other anomalies, with a
commentary on the play of mind in perception and art / by Roger N. Shepard.
    p.   cm.
1. Optical illusions. 2. Visual perception. I. Title.
QP495.S47 1990
152. 14'8— dc20   90-32451
ISBN 0-7167-2134-1   C I P
ISBN 0-7167-2133-3 (pbk.)

Printed in the United States of America

1 2 3 4 5 6 7 8 9 0   R R D   9 9 8 7 6 5 4 3 2 1

MIND SIGHTS

for Barbaranne

TABLE OF CONTENTS

ACKNOWLEDGMENTS

This book grew out of a series of ink drawings of illusions, ambiguities, and other visual anomalies that I began, originally for my own recreation, over 15 years ago. Some friends and associates suggested that many people would enjoy these visual puns, puzzles, and posers. Some suggested, further, that a written commentary on the pictures and on what they tell us about perception and the human mind could make the book a useful supplementary text in college or university courses on perception, psychology, or art.

Many people have encouraged or helped me toward the publication of this book. First and foremost is my wife, Barbaranne, who has been the strongest and most enduring supporter of the project during its long period of gestation; it is to her that this book is lovingly dedicated. Also greatly valued has been the encouragement of our three (now grown) children, Newland, Todd, and Shenna. Others who at one time or another have encouraged me to think that my drawings might be of interest to a wider public include Ernst Gombrich, Richard Gregory, Douglas Hofstadter, Scott Kim, Itsuo Sakane, and several of my former students and research associates, including Lynn Cooper, Jennifer Freyd, and the former Sherryl Judd.

I was first persuaded to write a commentary to accompany the drawings by Percy Diaconis and by Patricia Williams. I completed a first draft while I was Fowler Hamilton Visiting Research Fellow at Christ Church, Oxford University. I have since received helpful comments on that and subsequent drafts, as well as on other aspects of the project, from Eve Clark, Philip Johnson-Laird, Stephen Kosslyn, Michael Kubovy, and Vilayanur Ramachandran. Dorothy Spencer of Read/Write Press arranged for publication of the book with W. H. Freeman, and secured the painstaking copy editing of Barbara Fishman and the elegant book-design work of Suzanne West. To Suzanne and her daughter, Penelope West, belongs the credit for putting the book in its final form. Throughout the preparation for publication with W. H. Freeman, I have become particularly indebted to Freeman's senior editor, Jonathan Cobb, who contributed enormously to its eventual form and successful completion—through his enthusiasm for the book, for his wise counsel concerning the organization of the text and selection of drawings, and for his insightful suggestions for improvements in the last few drafts. Project Editor Diane Maass and Art Director Mike Suh of W. H. Freeman were also of great help in ensuring that the book was in final form to go to press.

Finally, I acknowledge the support that I have continued to receive from Stanford University and from the National Science Foundation, during these last 15 years, for my scientific research and writing on human perception and cognition, some of which is described in this book.

RNS
January 1990
Stanford, California

MIND SIGHTS

I

FOREWORD

I

F O R E W O R D

VISUAL TRICKS IN SCIENCE AND ART

Visual illusions, ambiguous figures, and depictions of impossible objects are inherently fascinating. Their violations of our most ingrained and immediate interpretations of external reality grab us at a deep, unarticulated level. A vague disquiet moves us to give something a closer look. We then see that what is before us is very different from what it first appeared to be. The world that we have relied on for solidity and stability shudders and shifts unpredictably, as if in a dream. Continuing our scrutiny, we finally satisfy ourselves that the aberration was only in the eye of the beholder and not, after all, in the world beheld. Reality regains its former stability and composure—and we laugh. It is the laugh that follows a narrowly averted accident.[1]

---

[1] This and ensuing superscript numbers throughout the text correspond to numbered notes and references, assembled separately for Parts I, II, and III at the back of the book.

This book brings together a number of ink drawings I have done over the last 15 years in exploring ways in which the eye or, really, the mind behind the eye can be tricked into interpretive flips or mental somersaults. I began making these drawings purely as a recreational diversion from my more serious, scientific work. With time, however, I came to see connections between the visual traps I was setting in these drawings and some of the basic principles I was investigating in the laboratory as a research psychologist specializing in the study of visual and auditory perception and related mental processes—primarily the mental processes (now generally called *cognitive* processes) by which we acquire our knowledge about the world around us.

Indeed, such anomalous pictures might be regarded as probes, of a sort, of the human perceptual-cognitive system. Through the millions of generations of its evolution in the three-dimensional world, the visual system has become highly efficient at providing us with an accurate and reliable internal representation of what is going on in that world. What our experience gives us is, in a sense, the "illusion" of direct, unmediated access to the external world. Our perceptual experience of a stable, continuous, and enduring three-dimensional surrounding retains no trace of the prodigiously complex neuronal machinery that so swiftly constructs that experience. Nor are we aware of the shifting, intermittent, pointillistic, upside-down, curved, two-dimensional patterns of retinal excitation from which the machinery of the brain constructs our visual world.

The underlying information-processing machinery of our brains reveals something of its constructive operations only when challenged with visual displays specially contrived to deviate from the regularities that prevailed in the world of our ancestors. Natural selection has not had time to adapt our biological makeup to the demands increasingly placed on it by technological innovations. For example, because our visual system has evolved to compensate for variations in natural illumination, we readily recognize a familiar object whether it is seen in the (yellower) direct sunlight of midday, the (redder) direct sunlight toward sunset, or the (bluer) indirect sunlight scattered to an object in shade. But we may walk right past our own car when, in a parking lot at night, it is illuminated only by the quite different, artificial light emitted by sodium or mercury vapor lamps.[2]

For every situation, our perceptual system automatically applies its previously successful and now thoroughly entrenched methods of processing. If the situation is quite different from those encountered by our ancestors, however, this system may deliver up incorrect or conflicting interpretations. From an analysis of the conditions giving rise to such perceptual errors and confusions in the psychological laboratory, researchers seek an understanding of the information processing methods that have until now remained deeply hidden in the biology of the visual system. Part of such an understanding may come from a consideration of how the regularities of the natural world, in which we have evolved, may have shaped our methods of processing the visual information that comes to us from that world.

Consider, for example, how we correctly see objects as being at different distances from us in three-dimensional space. Somehow, our visual system must "compute" the distances of objects solely on the basis of relations between the optical images of such objects on the two-dimensional retinas at the backs of our eyes. The computation depends on such basic facts about the world as that light travels in straight lines. The geometry of straight-line projection has ensured virtually perfect correlations among certain relations between the images on the retina—sometimes called *retinal cues* to distance—and the actual distances of the corresponding objects.

An example of a relevant geometric fact is that the angle at one vertex of a right triangle will be smaller the farther the opposite side (of fixed length) is moved away from that vertex. Accordingly, for objects that are known to be of approximately equivalent actual sizes, such as two human adults, the more distant object will subtend a smaller visual angle at the eye. The smaller retinal image is therefore likely to be the image of the more distant object. This cue—of the relative sizes of retinal images—is called the *distance cue of retinal size*.

Moreover, regardless of the actual sizes of the two objects, the spatial relations between their projections will depend on the viewing position of the eye. From one position, the two objects will fall on the same line of sight and will therefore project to the same point on the retina. A small lateral movement of the viewing position will then break this alignment, with the image of the closer object moving left or right of the image of the farther object according to the direction of displacement of the viewpoint. Also, our two eyes view the world from positions that are laterally displaced with respect to each other. Therefore, a comparison of the relations between the projections of objects in the two images makes possible a determination of the distances of the corresponding objects in three-dimensional space. This is called the *distance cue of binocular parallax.*

Normally, all such retinal sources of information about the relative distances of objects in three-dimensional space are highly correlated with each other. Does the visual system use one source of information or cue and ignore another? Or does it combine the different sources in some way to arrive at its estimates of the distances? In the psychological laboratory, optical prisms, mirrors, projectors, polarizing filters, electronic shutters, and increasingly, computer-controlled display screens have made possible the independent variation of such previously correlated cues. By varying each retinally available source of information about distance independently, experimental psychologists seek to learn which sources of information or cues to distance our perceptual machinery actually uses in computing the distances of objects and how much each source is weighted in this computation.

We can then compare the results of such experiments with what is to be expected of a visual processing system that has arisen through random variation and natural selection in the real world. We might expect that the sources of information that would provide the most accurate and reliable information about distance would be most heavily weighted in such visual processing. For example, binocular parallax should dominate retinal size in determining the perceived distances of nearby objects because the use of parallax, unlike the use of retinal size, does not depend on (possibly erroneous) assumptions about the real sizes of the external objects themselves. Conversely, retinal size should dominate binocular parallax in determining the perceived distances of remote objects because binocular parallax necessarily loses its discriminatory power when the distance to the objects becomes very large relative to the distance between the two eyes.

Long before the establishment of psychology as an experimental science (little more than 100 years ago), artists and architects had for centuries been investigating human visual perception and the illusions to which it is susceptible. As far back as the classical period of Greek architecture, a few centuries B.C., temples such as the Parthenon were deliberately designed so that certain lines of the building, which through visual illusion would otherwise appear slightly curved in one direction, were curved in the opposite direction just enough to correct for the illusion and thus appear perfectly straight.[3] And during the much later Renaissance period, Roman artists and architects such as Michelangelo and Borromini in the fifteenth to seventeenth centuries were deliberately using illusions of perspective to create arcades and piazzas that appear deeper and grander than those that would otherwise have been possible within the constraints of available space and resources.[4]

Indeed, since the beginning of the Renaissance, the developments by graphic artists of such pictorial innovations as linear perspective (and then intentional violations of linear perspective), aerial perspective, trompe l'oeil, as well as the still later developments of impressionism, pointillism, cubism, surrealism, abstract expressionism, and optical ("op") art can each be regarded as a different kind of experimental challenge to the human visual system. In effect, these artists have constructed illusory, ambiguous, or impossible scenes by manipulating different sources of information available to the retina. Some of the better known of these experimenters in visual anomaly have been Leonardo da Vinci, William Hogarth, Pablo Picasso, Salvador Dali, Pavel Tchelitchew, Josef Albers, Victor Vasarely, Bridget Riley and particularly the late Dutch graphic artist Maurits Escher and the late Belgian surrealist painter René Magritte (the two to whose works my own efforts, reproduced in this book, bear perhaps the closest resemblance). The goal of these artists has not, however, been the objective and quantitative characterization of the way in which human responses depend on explicitly specified aspects of the visual stimulus. Rather, their primary goal has been the achievement of a subjective and qualitative experience that they value—and, hence, the achievement of a visual product (drawing, painting, sculpture, or building) that is capable of eliciting that valued experience within themselves (and, some of them hoped, within others).

Because the visual experiments of artists have been oriented toward a different goal, they have, in important respects, been much more freewheeling than the tightly controlled experiments of psychologists. Limited only by the reach of their unarticulated intuitions and visual sensibilities, artists have manipulated their visual materials in complex ways that are not yet reducible to the physically specifiable dimensions of the scientific laboratory. The unfettered explorations of artists have nevertheless been an important source of hypotheses for the ensuing, more methodical experiments of perceptual psychologists.

Recently, however, technological developments have provided perceptual researchers the kinds of freedom that were previously unavailable to artists. While painters had been able to distribute shapes, colors, and textures over a wall, canvas, or sheet of paper in any way they wished, the product remained a flat, two-dimensional surface. In striving to achieve the illusion of a three-dimensional scene, artists could manipulate only a subset of the normal cues to depth. In addition to the cue provided by the size of an image, they could manipulate such cues as linear and aerial perspective. Linear perspective is, in fact, related to the cue called retinal size, subtending smaller and smaller visual angles, converge to a vanishing point. In aerial perspective, very distant objects, such as mountains, appear lighter and bluer—that is, more like the sky itself—as a result of the short wavelengths of sunlight that are scattered back to the eye not by the distant objects themselves but by the molecules of the intervening atmosphere.

A painter could not, however, control the very powerful sources of information available to viewers who are free to choose the vantage points from which they subsequently view the painting. Thus, despite all the painter's efforts to portray a three-dimensional scene, the binocular parallax afforded by a viewer's two eyes would provide compelling information that the painting is, after all, only a two-dimensional surface. And, the same information is available even to a one-eyed viewer who is free to change viewing position over time—through the related information provided by motion parallax. In principle, the technological resources of the modern perceptual laboratory, including computer-generated stereographic displays and holograms, are now beginning to lead to a potentially more versatile and more visually compelling medium for art. Even so, most people undoubtedly remain, like artists, more interested in experiencing the subjective response that works of art can elicit within themselves than in studying the experimental findings and perceptual theories that emerge from psychological laboratories. Many of the people who visit art museums and galleries have little desire to peruse the journals in which experimental psychologists report their results on visual perception (just as many of the people who attend concerts or listen to recordings have little inclination to study musical scores or musicological treatises).

Partly for this reason, I had not initially planned to write anything beyond the briefest possible introduction to accompany my drawings. Several colleagues suggested, however, that many readers would be curious about how I came to produce such drawings and about what the effects that such anomalous pictures have on viewers can tell us about the human mind. Accordingly, I have written two separate sections: the remainder of the Foreword from my perspective as the artist and the Afterword from my perspective as a perceptual researcher.

In the following autobiographical note I offer some personal reflections on the developments of my penchant for drawing, my fascination with visual pranks and illusions, and my curiosity—first about machines, then about bodies, and finally about minds. I speculate that a number of these emerging tendencies seem to have converged both in my career in psychological science and in my drawings included here.

From my reflections on the origins of my drawings and how they fit into my work as a perceptual scientist, I move on to Part II, in which I present the drawings themselves. The drawings are organized into annotated groups according to the types of anomalies illustrated.

Finally, in Part III (the Afterword) I present an analysis of the types of visual tricks used in the different groups of drawings and then a more general discussion of perception, pictures, anomalies, and the mind. Although it is intended to be relatively nontechnical, this discussion may go further into issues of visual perception and graphic depiction than some readers may wish. It is partly for this reason (and partly so that I can refer back to the drawings as illustrations of particular visual tricks) that I have placed this analysis and discussion after the drawings. I believe that enjoyment of the drawings does not depend on reading the Afterword. Nevertheless, I hope that the drawings will stimulate some readers to consider what I have to say there about what visual anomalies tell us about the human mind.

An Early Impulse to Draw

Beginning in childhood, I vented through endless drawings what one of my despairing elementary school teachers termed my "feverish imagination." At one stage, my insatiable requirements for paper drove me to obtain the unused ends of rolls of newsprint from the publisher of the local daily paper. These early drawings typically portrayed vast, other-worldly vistas whose desolation was here and there broken by strange, solitary towers, futuristic vehicles, machines, robots, and much later (and to the extent that my skills grew adequate to the task), beautiful women.

Until I was persuaded to seek publication of the drawings contained in this book, however, my artistic endeavors remained a largely private and, with the mounting demands of my scientific career, an increasingly sporadic diversion. Of the drawings included here, only a few have appeared before—in a traveling exhibition in Japan,[5] in a few magazine articles,[6] and on a T-shirt.[7]

Otherwise, my graphic efforts have previously been published only in two forms. First, I submitted the four entries reproduced in Figure I-1 for a 1984 design contest for a logo for the Western Psychological Association. (The three-dimensional entry in the upper left was adopted by the association and now appears on its letterhead. My other three entries play on figure-ground ambiguity, which is a prominent feature of a number of the drawings featured in this book; the drawing in the upper

FIGURE I-1

*Four designs, playing with figure-ground organization, that I submitted to
the logo design contest of the Western Psychological Association (WPA).*

right also incorporates the standard symbol for psychology—the Greek letter *psi*.)

Second, I have usually done the illustrations for my own scientific papers and books. As a reflection of my turn of mind, these figures, like the theories I have proposed, the stimuli I have constructed, and the methods of data analysis I have developed, have often had a heavily geometric aspect. Figures I-2 and I-3 are illustrative examples.

An Early Fascination with Mechanisms

In addition to drawing, another of my early preoccupations was tinkering with mechanical gadgets. While I trace my penchant for drawing primarily to my mother, Grace Newland Shepard, who was an art major at Stanford and an artist in many media, including watercolor, weaving, and needlework; I trace my fascination with things mechanical principally to my father, O. Cutler Shepard, who rose through the ranks to professor and head of materials sciences in Stanford's School of Engineering. As a boy, he had built a gasoline-powered wagon, a crystal radio receiver, and from a beginner's Erector set, a derrick that won him the prize of an advanced Erector set. In any case, one of my earliest memories was the wonderful discovery, on my first tricycle expedition around the corner of our block, of an old clockwork and some other mechanical junk abandoned in a vacant lot. I later spent many happy hours tinkering with old mechanical phonographs, radios, crank telephones, and the like in the barn on my grandparents' San Jose prune and walnut orchard—as well as with the two Erector sets that my father passed on to me.

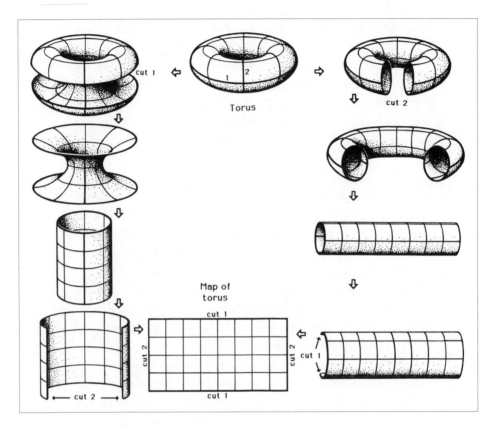

FIGURE 1-2

Illustration that I prepared for a paper that mathematician Eloise Carlton and I wrote. The drawing shows two ways in which a torus—a two-dimensional surface resembling the surface of a doughnut—can be cut and opened out into a flat rectangle, called the map of the torus.[10]

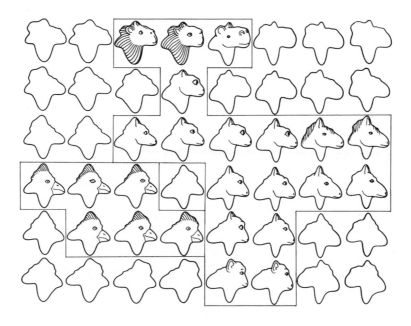

FIGURE 1-3

Computer-generated, free-form outline shapes that research collaborator Greg
Cermak and I presented to people in a study of perceptual interpretations of ambiguous figures, displayed here with internal markings that I subsequently added to some
of the outlines to illustrate one commonly reported type of perceptual interpretation—that of the head of an animal. Among the shapes that often were described as
the head of an animal facing to the right, frequently reported animals were a lion or
a hippo (for the shapes shown at the top in this array), a bird (for the shapes at the
left), a horse or large dog (for the shapes at the right), a bear or monkey (for the shapes
at the bottom), and a small dog, cat, or lamb (for the shapes in the central portion).
To illustrate the ambiguity of the empty outlines, near the center of the array I have
deliberately left blank one shape that might be perceptually interpreted as a bird facing right, as a lamb facing right, or as a large dog (such as a German shepherd)
facing left. (Adapted from Figure 9 on page 371 of R. N. Shepard and G. W.
Cermak, "Perceptual-cognitive explorations of a toroidal set of free-form stimuli,"
Cognitive Psychology 4 [1973]: 351-377.)

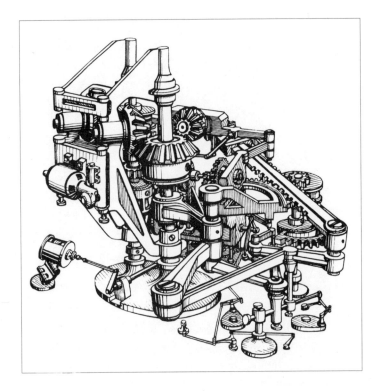

FIGURE 1-4

One of my drawings of imaginary mechanical assemblages.

Not surprisingly, my early drawings featured mechanical contrivances and conveyances: futuristic cars, powerboats, interplanetary rockets, and (I now shamefacedly confess) horrendous machines of conquest and destruction. Later, my gradually maturing interest in science and technology manifested itself in the pictorial creation of colossal instruments of, for that time, advanced science—Van de Graaff electrostatic generators, atom smashers, astronomical telescopes, and more and more intricately articulated mechanical assemblages (for an example, see Figure I-4)—including automatons that, if not exactly wearing their hearts on their sleeves, afforded inner glimpses of their animating motors, shafts, gears, racks, pinions, cranks, cams, and linkages.

Robots intrigued me as the ultimate in sophisticated mechanical devices. Between the ages of 10 and 16, I even went so far as to build some motorized robots. The first of these, animated by reversible electric motors taken from a toy train and from the horn of a 1920s automobile, had a casing soldered together from tin cans, was able to grasp ferrous objects by means of small electromagnets removed from an old door bell, and rolled about on a base housed in a small wooden cheese box (Figure I-5, left). The last and most ambitious of these, a 5-foot, aluminum-clad robot, walked erect on parallelogram-action legs powered by a reciprocating motor salvaged from a discarded washing machine (Figure I-5, right). Although less anthropomorphic, two other robotic devices, which I built during this same period, went further in emulating specific sensory and motor capabilities. One was a crude sonar device, distantly akin to those now used in some security alarm systems (and, of course, by bats and dolphins) that could detect the

FIGURE I-5

Two electromechanical robots designed and built in my youth.

close approach of a person or other large object by means of reflected sound waves. The other was a servo-mechanically operated pen for electrically reproducing writing or drawing as it was being executed at a distant location.

This early preoccupation with robots and other machines that could perform human functions may have been the first manifestation of the search for the mechanisms underlying perception, thought, and behavior that has driven my research ever since I dedicated myself to a career in psychological science almost 40 years ago.

A Penchant for Perceptual Pranks

That so much of my psychological research has focused specifically on perception and imagery may be partially traceable to another tendency that emerged early—namely, an uncommon delight in contriving perceptual tricks, pranks, and illusions. The types of pranks that especially appealed to me were those whose essential elements were perceptual incongruity and surprise.

I would sometimes go to considerable lengths just to precipitate one brief moment of bafflement in the chosen victim. Thus, while my sister was still downstairs one evening, I used her rug to noiselessly slide every article of furniture and every appurtenance (including drapes, pictures, clothing, and the rug itself) from her bedroom, down the hall, and into another room, so that when she went up for bed, she confronted a completely bare room. Of course, I thereby incurred stern parental admonishment—as well as an injunction to restore everything immediately to its former place. But, even so, the effect that I had so fleetingly achieved seemed worth all the labors of preparation and restitution.

Occasionally, even relatively simple preparations yielded satisfactory results. After finally getting around to following my mother's repeated request to put my own room in order, I carefully positioned a full-length mirror on a stand just behind where the door to my room opened. I was soon rewarded by my mother's startled gasp as, on attempting to enter my room (presumably to check on my compliance with her request), she found herself about to collide with another woman, equally determinedly leaving.

In rare instances, I was also greatly regaled by surprising flukes that arose without intentional preparation. One evening, during a large family gathering, my father and I arranged all the available chairs for an after-dinner slide show. Everyone was seated in the living room facing the front door, where we customarily placed the projection screen. My father was just about to set up the screen when a timorous young man, having finally screwed up his courage to ask my sister for a date, rang the door bell. Upon the opening of the door, the unfortunate young man found himself under the scrutiny of not only the girl's father but also row upon row of expectantly seated aunts, uncles, cousins, and grandparents.

Sometimes preparations, though intentional, led to unexpectedly amusing turns of events. One night, I picked up a friend in my parents' enormous 1937 Buick Roadmaster (the sort of car favored by gangsters, according to movies of the period). After affixing to my face a grotesquely large but otherwise remarkably realistic papier-mâché nose I had made, we drove off in search of adventure. We soon noticed a man waiting alone at a bus stop. Pulling over, I called out a question about directions. The man stepped forward to answer but, on gaining his first full view of my face in the light of the street lamp, visibly blanched and took a step back, wordless. It was as if he had suffered a physical blow. I drove away slowly, and some five to ten minutes later I again brought the car toward the same bus stop. By this time, several other people had gathered there, and the originally solitary man had evidently come to the realization that he had been the victim of a prank. On recognizing our car, he stepped out from the group, and presumably to show us that he had not, after all, been taken in, he loudly shouted, "Blow your nose!" He had not waited long enough to see that since our preceding encounter I had removed the false nose. Slowing, I pulled closer as if to see why on earth this stranger had shouted such an absurdity and thereby clearly revealed in the light of the street lamp the normal but quite puzzled faces of my friend and myself. Once again, the hapless man found himself retreating from the road—but this time to face (as my friend and I drove off for the last time) the equally puzzled looks of the others waiting for the bus.

My closest high school friend Kenneth Harmon and I were particularly given to perpetrating perceptual pranks—not only on our families and schoolmates but also on each other. One noon, while I was getting my lunch out of the trunk of the car, Ken, on a sudden inspiration, unscrewed the round cream-colored knob from the floor-mounted stick shift and, forfeiting a portion of his lunch, carefully impaled on the now-knobless stick a freshly peeled hard-boiled egg. After restarting the engine, I grasped the knob in an attempt to shift into first gear. The resulting tactual sensation can only be described as indescribable.

Years later I had a fortuitous opportunity to try something similar on my recent bride. One morning, my wife Barbaranne used one of our coffee cups to hold the maple syrup she had heated for our pancakes. Noticing that her cup of black, unsweetened coffee and the cup of heated syrup were visually indistinguishable, I effected a hasty switch while she was off fetching the pancakes. I only wish I could have a photograph of her expression as she took her first sip of what she supposed was her coffee.

Such moments, in which perceptual experience totally fails to mesh with expectation, produce a peculiar internal state of epistemological dislocation. One suddenly knows that something has gone radically wrong with the world but has not the slightest inkling what. Something of this sort later befell me when I unwittingly ran our power mower over a hornets' nest.

With the responsibilities of fatherhood and a professional career, I exercised my penchant for practical jokes less frequently and in a form that became more restrained and generally more conceptual than perceptual. The most recent example was based on my earlier publication, with my then-graduate student Jackie Metzler, of what has come to be (through its coverage in introductory psychology textbooks) my single most widely known paper—namely, a 1971 paper in the journal *Science* that introduced the experimental study of "mental rotation." [8]

In this experiment, we presented people with pairs of the perspective views of three-dimensional objects in different orientations in space shown in Figure I-6. We measured the time the people took to decide whether the two objects in each pair were identical in shape despite their differences in orientation or were intrinsically different

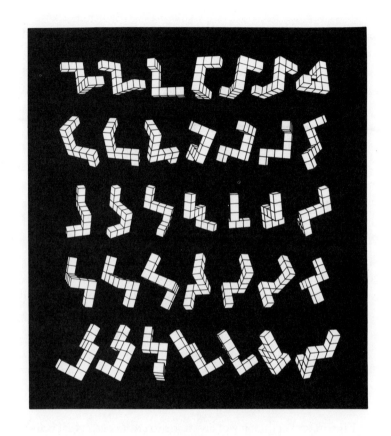

FIGURE 1-6

The computer-generated three-dimensional objects that I used in my first study, with Jacqueline Metzler, of "mental rotation."[8] (Originally appeared on the cover of the February 19, 1971, issue of the journal Science.)

in shape—in which case they were mirror-image shapes, like a left and a right hand. The decision time increased linearly with the angular difference in the portrayed orientations of the two objects. We concluded that the subjects had to imagine one object rotating into congruence with the other object and that they could imagine this rotation at a rate of no more than about 60° per second.

The opportunity for the prank came many years later, when my daughter Shenna was searching for an experimental project to do during her senior year at Tufts University. I persuaded her to try an experiment on mental rotation and to enlist the assistance, in carrying out the statistical analyses, of a young faculty member at the University of Pittsburgh by the name of Douglas Metzler. Although no relation to my former student, Jackie Metzler, Douglas Metzler had previously corresponded with me about my research on mental rotation. Shenna carried out her experiment so successfully that it was published on its own merits in the *Journal of Experimental Psychology*.[9] I have since enjoyed the confusion occasioned by the appearance of a second Shepard-Metzler paper on mental rotation—by a different Shepard and a different Metzler.

Toward a Systematic Pursuit of Illusion

Even in my youth, some of my efforts to create perceptual befuddlement were more disciplined—and also more welcomed—than my practical jokes. In particular, I presented occasional magic shows. My lack of natural flair for showmanship was partially offset by my success in the offstage design and construction of trick cabinets for effecting the appearance and disappearance of various objects. My interest in violating one of the most fundamental of our internalized cognitive/ perceptual principles, the principle of conservation of material objects, may have been another premonitory indication of my later turn toward the more serious study of perception and cognition. (Incidentally, the experiment that I was initially assigned as a first-year graduate student at Yale was concerned not with perception in humans but with learning in rats. But, as someone once quipped, while a magician may pull a rabbit out of a hat, a psychologist can pull a habit out of a rat.)

Foreshadowing still more closely my eventual investigations into visual perception, I constructed what I later found to be known as a *pseudoscope*—an optical device in which an arrangement of four mirrors effectively interchanges the left and right viewpoints of the two eyes (Figure I-7). The pseudoscope was one of the early devices that enabled researchers to control different retinal cues to depth separately. By reversing binocular parallax, the pseudoscope yields apparent inversions in depth in which (unfamiliar) convex objects look concave, concave objects look convex, and in which any movement of the viewer's head induces, in such perceptually inverted objects, the illusion of an astonishing twisting motion. (Such a device also demonstrates the power of perceptual learning. A particularly familiar convex object—the human face—does not reverse its apparent depth when viewed through the pseudoscope.) Figure I-8 shows how the illusion provided by the pseudoscope can be experienced, without the aid of special apparatus, by simply closing one eye and thus eliminating the cue of binocular parallax.

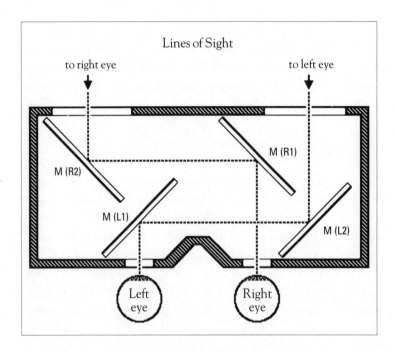

FIGURE I-7

Basic plan of a pseudoscope. Four mirrors are so positioned that they reverse the left-eye and right-eye views of the world. As a consequence, the apparent concavity or convexity of many three-dimensional objects viewed through the pseudoscope appear reversed in depth.

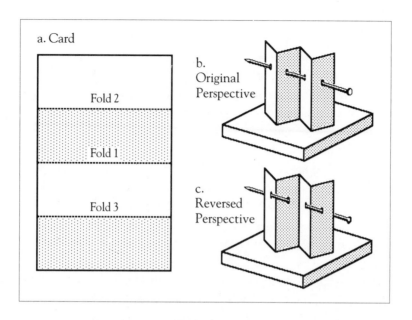

FIGURE 1-8

A way in which a card might be folded and viewed (most effectively through one eye) so that the resulting shape can be perceptually reversed in depth and then seen to rotate when the head is moved. To try this, fold a small rectangular piece of heavy paper, or 3"x 5" index card, into the form of a W, along three parallel lines as indicated in a. Then stand the folded card on a horizontal surface, such as the flat palm of your extended hand or a table top, as indicated in b, in such a way that none of the four folded rectangular sections is blocked from view by any of the others. While viewing it at arm's length through one eye, try to see the folded shape as reversed in depth, as indicated in c. (I have tried to make clear the depth interpretations intended in b and c by indicating how a knitting needle might be expected to pierce the folded sections of the card in the two cases.) The reversal, which may take a while to attain, can usually be facilitated by focusing on a back corner of the folded shape while trying to imagine it instead as a front corner. As soon as the experience of inverted depth has been achieved, a side-to-side head motion will cause the shape to appear to undergo an autonomous rotating motion of its own.

My pursuit of perceptual illusions has continued into my current scientific research on phenomena of visual and auditory perception. In the visual domain, one of the principal phenomena that I have been investigating is the illusion known as *visual apparent motion*. In this illusion, the alternating visual display of two similarly shaped objects in different positions gives rise to the appearance of a single object moving back and forth over a particular connecting path. This phenomenon attracted my attention as a striking perceptual manifestation of two deeply internalized mental principles. The first is the already mentioned principle of *object conservation*, which favors the perceptual interpretation that a single object moved from one location to another over the interpretation that one object went out of existence and a second object materialized in a different location. The second is a still more remarkable principle of mental traversal of the *kinematically simplest path*. According to the latter principle, the mentally interpolated motion between alternate presentations of the same object in different orientations in space is generally not along a straight path but along a certain helical curve uniquely prescribed by kinematic geometry.[10]

My explorations in the auditory domain began when I joined the technical staff of the Bell Telephone Laboratories in 1958. There, powerful computers first became available to me, and Max Mathews was developing the first general-purpose computer programs for the synthesis of musical sounds. With these new tools in 1963 I devised an auditory illusion of endlessly rising tones. Each successive tone is heard, unmistakably, as one step higher in pitch on the chromatic scale than the tone heard before it. But because the continuing sequence actually passes through an endlessly repeating cycle, no matter how long the apparently rising sequence is continued, it never in fact gets any higher.[11] This tonal illusion later led me to the study of auditory phenomena of ambiguity and apparent motion (mentioned in the Afterword) that are quite analogous to the already mentioned visual phenomena of ambiguity and apparent motion.

A Turn Inward Toward the Mental

Although some precursors to my later psychological interests may be discernible in my earlier period of preoccupation with visual effects and robotic devices, throughout my youth I nevertheless remained set on a career in physical science. Before I turned toward a career in psychological science, my interests developed in some new directions.

Developmental surveys have in fact found evidence that as boys mature their expressed career interests often shift from those primarily oriented toward physical objects and activities toward those more oriented toward people. Thus boys who had once said they wanted to be policemen, firemen, racing car drivers, air force pilots, astronauts, engineers, or physicists later said that they planned to go into entertainment, politics, business, law, medicine, or psychology. Shifts in the opposite direction, apparently, are relatively rare.

Perhaps the first indication of a shift of this kind in my own case was the emergence in my drawings of more softly curved and comely creatures. They must have appeared quite incongruous in the alien, angular, geometric, and mechanical settings in which they found themselves. I then entered a protracted period during which I seem to

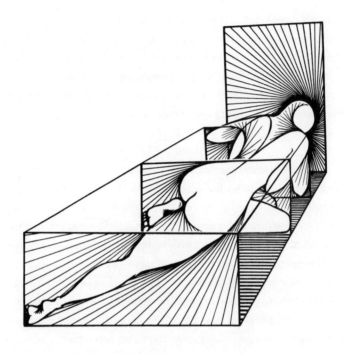

FIGURE I-9

One of my drawings that explored the mechanical or —in this case—abstract, geometric aspects of bodies.

have been exploring the geometric aspects of bodies. (Figure I-9 is a representative example.)

In any event, the path by which I approached psychological science does seem to have been by way of successive shifts in my curiosity from machines, to bodies, and then to minds. Minds, unlike machines and bodies, do not take a visible form. To the extent that one "knows one's own mind," one's knowledge of that mind is a private and subjective thing. To the extent that one knows other minds, one's knowledge of those minds is necessarily based on the behaviors of corresponding bodies over time. A mind itself is not the sort of thing that can be captured in a static depiction—though the portrayal of a posture (or a facial expression) that normally arises only in the course of a movement or action may achieve the illusion of animation[12] and hence of mindfulness.

The shift in my own principal preoccupation from bodies to minds eventually found pictorial expression of a quite different sort. Instead of attempting to depict mind through the external appearances of mindful bodies, I attempted to externalize the inner products of the mind itself. The "inner products" that especially attracted my attention were those that were sufficiently visual that they could in principle be rendered in the form of a physical picture that would cause a viewer to experience something close to the original inner experience. I attempted such externalizations of images of many different types, including, for example, the meaningless shifting patterns that arise in the closed eyes, either spontaneously or as the result of mechanical pressure applied to the eyeball; the occasional isolated face, scene, or geometric pattern that may vividly flash before the mind during the transition into or out of sleep; the dreams that in the depths of sleep are taken to be the unfolding of real events; the geometric patterns or bizarre visions that sometimes arise when the brain is affected by sleep deprivation, fever, or drugs; and the enormous variety of everyday mental images that may accompany or even constitute thinking, planning, remembering, and daydreaming—whether these images arise consciously, in a deliberate effort to solve a particular practical problem, or unconsciously.

As I entered young adulthood, I began to produce a large number of drawings, paintings, collages, and poems whose most salient aspects were their grotesque, surrealistic quality and their evident psychosexual symbolism. Most of the bizarre drawings that I produced during this period were not intended as accurate re-creations of particular images that I had spontaneously experienced in dreaming or other states. Nevertheless, they often either were inspired by spontaneous images that must in part have had an unconscious source or, if they arose through a free play of waking imagery or drawing, must have fascinated me because they engaged some deep-lying unconscious schemas within myself. Moreover, I soon thereafter found myself moved to attempt the accurate pictorial externalization of specific, particularly vivid or memorable scenes from my own nocturnal dreams. Incidentally, just as I have long been prone to thinking up perceptual pranks to play on others, part of my own brain, working unbeknownst to me during sleep, seems bent on surreptitiously conjuring up similar surprises for me. In one (of many) such dream incidents, I picked up from a table a hefty volume on eating out around the world. As I began idly thumbing through the book, it fell open to the title page for a chapter, "Tips on Dining Out in Central Africa." I turned the page and, across the following two-page spread, found only the huge bold-faced admonishment, "DON'T EAT THE FOOD."

My efforts toward the faithful externalization of particular, spontaneous visual images began in earnest following my involuntary experience of an extraordinarily vivid and geometrically regular visual image just before awakening one morning in 1970. Images that arise in the transition from sleep to wakefulness are called *hypnopompic* images (in contrast to *hypnagogic* images, which arise in the transition from wakefulness into sleep). With eyes still closed on that morning, I suddenly saw before me an immense, luminously shimmering, golden array of diamond-shaped panels separated by burnished beveled strips. Each panel contained one of two regular arrays of small black arrows or spadelike forms that were identical except for the direction in which these forms pointed, which was uniformly upward or to the left, in alternating panels. The vision lasted for what I retrospectively estimated to have been several seconds, until I became fully awake. Even then, my memory of the image remained so vivid and my feeling of awe at its vast scale, its pristine regularity, and its preternaturally luminous and shimmering quality remained so keen that I immediately set about making a pencil sketch of it together with notations as to its colors and other details. I then used this annotated sketch as the basis for a larger-scale, full-color reconstruction. A sense of the geometric regularity of the image can be gained from the black-and-white approximation included as

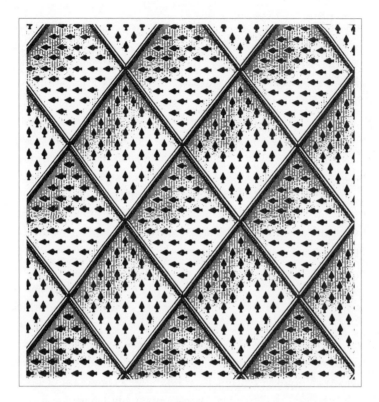

FIGURE I-10

A reconstruction of the geometrically regular hypnopompic image that I experienced for a few seconds just before awakening on the morning of December 27, 1970. This black-and-white sketch is necessarily a crude approximation, at best, to the pristine, infinite, and shimmering golden image that I experienced on that morning.

Figure I-10. Similar black-and-white versions of my reconstructions of five other such geometrically regular hypnopompic images, spontaneously experienced on subsequent occasions, are included in the Afterword. Full-color reproductions of all six original reconstructions are available in an earlier publication.[13]

Later I learned that some 100 years before, the eminent British astronomer, chemist, and co-inventor of photography, Sir John Herschel, had described similarly regular images that he had experienced on several occasions, particularly after he had been administered chloroform as a general anesthetic. Herschel described his images as "dazzling," as possessing "perfect symmetry and geometrical regularity," and as containing repeating complex "close patterns" or "filigree work." In light of the form of my own most memorable hypnopompic image (Figure I-10), I was particularly struck by Herschel's further remark that in "the great majority of instances" the geometrically regular visions he experienced took the form of "rhombic lattice works," with "the larger axes of other rhombs being vertical."[14]

Many scientists and creative thinkers have noted that the mind's best work is sometimes done without conscious direction, during receptive states of reverie, idle meditation, dreaming, or transition between sleep and wakefulness. In my case, the hypnopompic transition from sleep to wakefulness seems to have been the most productive not only of geometrically regular images but also of new artistic and scientific ideas. In particular, the idea for my original experiment with Jackie Metzler on mental rotation came to me (just before awakening) in the form of a dynamic hypnopompic image of three-dimensional objects majestically turning in space.[15] The perspective views of such objects, as they were later generated on the computer for the purposes of our experiment, are those already shown in Figure I-6.[16] This may have been the first instance of computer-assisted externalization of hypnopompic mental imagery.

Origin of the Present Drawings

The series of ink drawings presented in Part II of this book similarly began with a spontaneous image. The anomalous elephant reproduced on the cover took form in my mind as I was in the process of awakening early one morning in 1974. The quick pencil sketch that I made as soon as I was fully awake then served as a basis for the final ink drawing included here. The spontaneous emergence of this anomalous image then piqued my recently dormant curiosity about the relation of art and creativity to visual perception and the human mind. In the context of a course that I was then teaching at Stanford on perception, imagery, and thought, the resulting resurgence of my interest in visual anomalies predisposed me toward experiencing further images of this kind and toward externalizing them as drawings.

Many of the visual tricks that I exploit in my drawings were also inspired by the works of earlier artists—particularly Escher and Magritte. (Indeed, I would be pleased if my drawings were seen to combine some of the recursive, geometric qualities of Escher's black-and-white lithographs with some of the humor and whimsy of Magritte's paintings. Many of my drawings were actually done, however, before the works of these two artists had become widely known in the United States and, in some cases, before I had encountered the particular works that my drawings most closely resemble.) While some of my images arose (as the anomalous elephant) during the process of awakening, others emerged during evenings while I was doodling or playfully rearranging previous sketches. Now and again, a new image simply leapt out at me from a fortuitous configuration or alignment of unrelated environmental objects or shadows, or from a shift of attention from objects to the shapes of the spaces between objects.

An especially clear example of the way environmental objects can suggest perceptual anomalies is provided by another incident from my high school days. My friend Ken Harmon, espying a rabbit grazing on the lawn (appearing somewhat as I have sketched in Figure I-11), exclaimed, "Look, there's a duck on its back!" A number of years later,

FIGURE I-11

I learned that the duck-rabbit ambiguity was well-known in psychological circles, after having appeared as an illustration in a 1900 book by the psychologist Joseph Jastrow.[17] (It also became familiar in philosophical circles, after a simplified version appeared in Ludwig Wittgenstein's profoundly influential work *Philosophical Investigations*.[18]) It may take a magician to pull a rabbit out of a hat, but we all possess sufficient magic to pull a duck out of a rabbit.

An appreciable fraction of my life has already passed since I began doing these ink-drawn visual anomalies over 15 years ago, and nothing short of death may bring the fitful process of their augmentation to a close. I have accordingly been persuaded that I should not wait any longer to present a selection of the drawings that are already completed. The selection included in Part II represents a convergence—and, I hope, the attainment of a satisfactory balance—between the unfettered self-expression of my earlier artistic efforts and the more disciplined restraint of my later scientific endeavors.

II

THE DRAWINGS

II

THE DRAWINGS

INTRODUCTION

I have arranged my drawings into nine groups, each featuring a different type of visual anomaly. I give each of these nine types a letter designation and a brief descriptive name: (A) depth illusions, (B) depth ambiguities, (C) object ambiguities, (D) figure-ground ambiguities, (E) figure-ground impossibilities, (F) depth impossibilities, (G) pictorial self-reference, (H) symbolic self-reference, and (I) transmogrification. Some of the drawings illustrate more than one of these nine types of anomaly. Consequently, my assignment of each drawing to one particular group is sometimes a bit arbitrary.

In the group illustrating *illusion*, the drawings give rise to perceptual interpretations that differ in some surprising way from what can objectively be found to be true of the physical patterns of the pictures themselves. In the groups labeled *ambiguity*, each drawing supports two or more mutually incompatible perceptual interpretations, only one of which is fully experienced at a time. In the groups designated *impossibility*, different parts of each drawing unambiguously give rise to perceptual interpretations that are incompatible with each other and thereby preclude the achievement of a stable percept of a three-dimensional object or scene as a whole. In the *self-reference* groups, the drawings in some way reproduce, represent, or refer back to themselves. And in the group dubbed *transmogrification*, each drawing is interpreted not just as a certain object, but also as an interpretation-altering transformation of that object. Altogether, I distinguish nine groups rather than five to allow separate consideration of anomalies of the same general type that arise in different ways. For example, ambiguity or impossibility can arise from depth or from figure-ground organization, and self-reference can arise from pictorial or from symbolic interpretation.

For convenience in referring to individual drawings, each drawing is designated both by a short and, I hope, memorable name and by its ordinal position (for example, 1, 2, or 3) in its group (for example, A, B, or C). As an introduction to the drawings, I first present an array of my depictions of arches to illustrate the various types of anomaly.

ARCHETYPAL ANOMALIES

DEPTH ILLUSION

DEPTH AMBIGUITY

FIGURE-GROUND AMBIGUITY

FIGURE-GROUND IMPOSSIBILITY

ARCHETYPAL ANOMALIES

DEPTH IMPOSSIBILITY

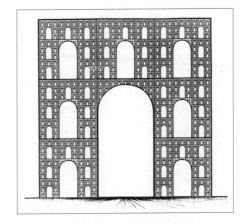

PICTORIAL SELF-REFERENCE

SYMBOLIC SELF-REFERENCE

TRANSMOGRIFICATION

A

DEPTH ILLUSIONS

Depth illusions are induced by the depth interpretation that we impose on a visual display. The perceptually reversible folded card illustrated in Figure I-8 is an example of a depth illusion (as well as of a depth ambiguity). The visual displays considered in this section, however, are flat, two-dimensional depictions of possible three-dimensional scenes.

Because we are generally unaware that we are imposing a perceptual interpretation on the stimulus, we are generally unaware that our experience has an illusory aspect. The illusory aspect may strike us only after we are informed, for example, that the sizes or shapes of lines or areas that appear very unequal are, in fact, identical in the picture. For this reason, the visual illusions that I present, unlike most of the other anomalies, are often accompanied by a short text that specifies which parts of the drawing are identical in size or shape. Such a statement can most compellingly be verified by carefully tracing the outline of one specified part on a thin sheet of paper and then sliding the tracing paper over the drawing to check for congruence of the outline with the other specified part of the drawing. Many of these illusions are discussed in more detail in the Afterword.

Although three of my examples of illusion (Drawings A4, A5, and A6) are also examples of depth ambiguity, I have included them here (rather than in Group B) because in these drawings the illusions to which the ambiguities give rise are more striking than the ambiguities themselves.

A1 TERROR SUBTERRA

*(With apologies to Latin scholars.) The two monsters are identical in size.
In addition to seeing them as different in size, do we also interpret their identical faces as expressing different emotions—such as rage on the part of the
pursuer and fear on the part of the pursued?*

A2 TURNING THE TABLES

The tops of the two tables are of identical size and shape in the plane of the picture. (This drawing is an elaboration of a parallelogram illusion that I first published in 1981.)[1]

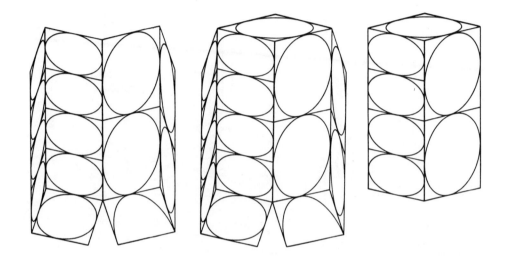

A3 UNCERTAIN CIRCLES

This is the first of three examples of illusions that depend on which of two depth interpretations is imposed on an ambiguous figure. Here, the same curves inscribed in the parallelograms may appear either as circles or as elongated or flattened ellipses. One depth interpretation is favored by ignoring the topmost parallelogram in the drawing; the other interpretation is favored by ignoring the parallelograms along the sides and bottom.

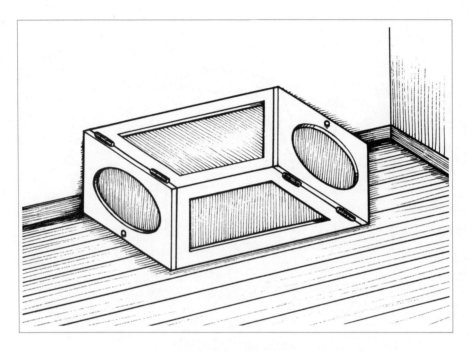

A4 MAGICIAN'S CABINET

This, too, is an ambiguous picture in which a perceptual illusion depends on the depth interpretation imposed. If the right end of the cabinet is seen as truncated at an odd angle to the rest of the cabinet and as fitted with a (closed) door viewed from the outside of the cabinet, then that door appears to be square with a circular window. Alternatively, if the right end of the cabinet is interpreted as parallel to the left end of the cabinet and fitted with a door viewed from the inside (as if the top and front panels of the cabinet were removed), then that door appears to be rectangular with an elliptical window.

A5 WRONG-WAY ARCH

We seem to be looking down on a road passing under a strangely skewed arch. More-over, the perspective seems weirdly reversed, with the vanishing point of the road (and of the arch) in the foreground rather than in the distance. If we ignore the road, how-ever, we may reverse the perspective interpretation of the arch. We may then see it as an essentially normal, rectangular structure, which we are looking up at from inside. What was the roof (from the former viewpoint) now becomes the ceiling of the build-ing, and what was the closest edge of the roof (the line just above the words TURN BACK) now becomes the farthest edge of the ceiling.

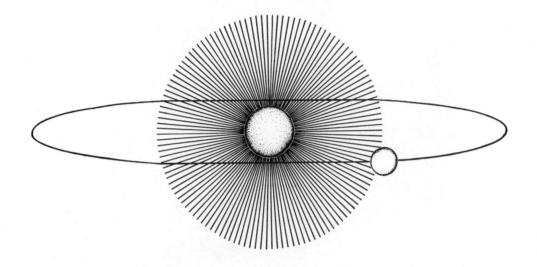

A6 GRAVITATIONAL BENDING

This drawing illustrates a depth illusion to the extent that the portrayed orbit of the planet is interpreted as circular, even though the projection of a circular orbit must of course be elliptical in the picture plane. In addition, this drawing illustrates a second, more remarkable illusion. The two portions of the planetary orbit that overlap the circular disk of rays emanating from the central sun are not even elliptical. In fact, those two horizontal portions are exactly straight. The two straight segments appear curved (as if they were portions of an ellipse) because they are superimposed on the field of radiating lines, just as in an illusion presented by the German physiologist Ewald Hering in 1861.[2]

B

The drawings classified as *depth ambiguities* are, again, ambiguous with respect to the depth interpretation of the portrayed three-dimensional object or scene. Each ambiguity arises because the object or scene is portrayed from a viewing position that yields special alignments or congruences of shape in the resulting two-dimensional image. In the first drawing of this group (B1), the alternative interpretations are made explicit by displacement of parts of the object (the hinged doors) away from their peculiar alignments relative to the special viewpoint. In the second drawing (B2), the alternative interpretations are made explicit by the placement of additional objects (the adventuresome rabbits). In the remainder of the drawings, the alternative perceptual interpretations are left as an exercise for the viewer.

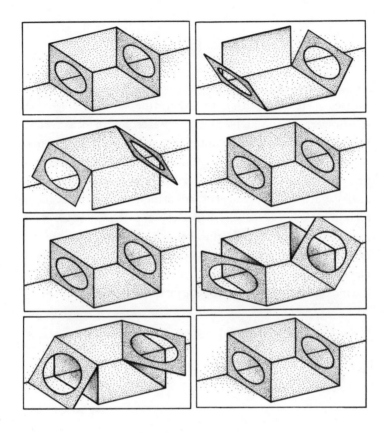

B1 OPEN-AND-SHUT CASE

This more schematic variant of the Magician's Cabinet *(Drawing A4) opens its doors to reveal further magical transformations. In addition to being capable of assuming different shapes, the cabinet or "case" is capable of transporting itself from the floor to the ceiling.*

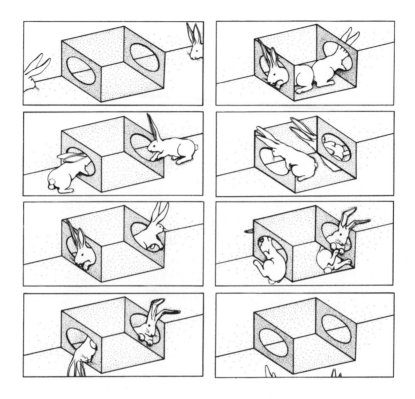

B2 RAREBITS OF ADVENTURE

Here, the magical transformations of the Magician's Cabinet are experienced by two inquisitive bunnies. In the next-to-last panel on the right, once the cabinet is seen as displaced to the ceiling, the bunnies appear to be barely holding on. In the last panel, only the tips of their ears are visible as, having lost their grips, the unfortunate bunnies fall out of sight.

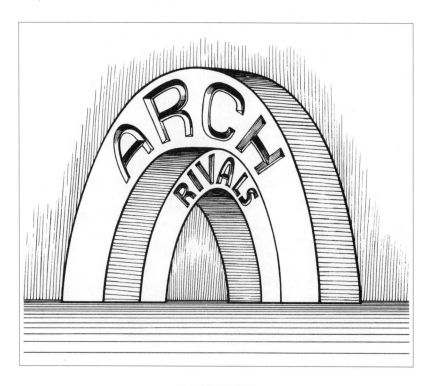

B3 ARCH RIVALS

B4 SISTER RIVALS

Normality here depends on seeing two faces rather than one.

B5 EGYPTIAN-EYEZED TÊTE-À-TÊTE

The case here is the reverse of that of the preceding drawing, B4: normality now depends on seeing one face rather than two. (This drawing also illustrates figure-ground ambiguity.)

B6 REFLECTING PRINCE

As in the earlier Sister Rivals (Drawing B4), normality here depends on seeing two faces rather than one—in this case, one in which the (perhaps extraterrestrial) "prince" has his hands raised in "reflection," or prayer.

C

OBJECT AMBIGUITIES

Object ambiguity refers to something that although not ambiguous with respect to either its global structure in depth or its organization into figure and ground can nevertheless be perceived as either of two (or more) quite distinct objects. An earlier example was the duck-rabbit illustrated in Figure I-11. As in all types of ambiguity, the effect is most compelling when the alternative interpretations are mutually exclusive and so cannot be experienced at the same time.

Often, in object ambiguities, the alternative perceptual interpretations are associated with different perceived orientations of the object. Thus, whereas the rabbit in Figure I-11 is perceived as on its feet and facing down, the duck is perceived as on its back and facing up. Indeed, for all the ambiguous objects in the present group (C)—except the *IV* in *Four In Five* (Drawing C4)—the alternative interpretations are differentially favored by viewing the drawing in different orientations.

C1 GLEE TURNS GLUM

Notice that Glee remains at the top and Glum on the bottom even when the whole picture is turned upside down.

C2 ONE TO THREE

Notice how different contexts favor different interpretations of the same character. For example, the w of Two is also the E of ONE and the 3 of 0123. (In addition, the middle word of the title might be ambiguously interpreted as to or as two.)

C3 ZERO THROUGH FOUR

As with Drawing C2, the middle word of this title can be alternatively taken in at least two ways—including the sense of "through the centers of the four other number names."

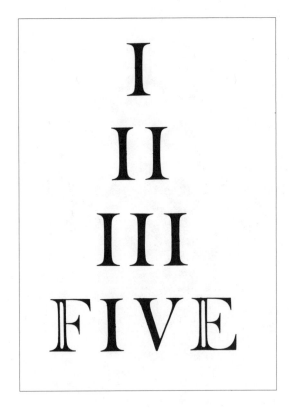

C4 FOUR IN FIVE

Once again, the middle word of the title has a quite literal interpretation.

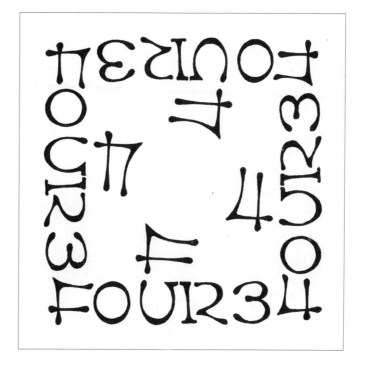

C5 FOUR SQUARED

C6 ZEN AND THE ART OF CYCLE MAINTENANCE

My title was, of course, inspired by Robert Pirsig's book, Zen and the Art of
Motorcycle Maintenance.[3]

a jagged edge
pegged padded
baggage agape

C7 CONVEYOR ERROR HORROR

Here, I have used seven different positions of one shape to form all seven of the letters (namely, a, b, d, e, g, j, and p) in the sentence describing the "horror"—much as four orientations distinguish the four standard letters b, d, p, and q . In case the sentence describing the "horror" proves too difficult to read, a translation is given in the Afterword. (Compliments to Scott Kim, author of Inversions,[4] who originally introduced me to the letter shape used here, when he formed most of the letters of my own name from this shape.)

D

FIGURE-GROUND AMBIGUITIES

Perhaps the most familiar type of ambiguous figure is that in which, upon a perceptual reversal, what was the background pops out as the figure and what was the figure vanishes into the background. An example shown in the Foreword was the WPA logo in the lower right of Figure I-1, where either the white *p* is seen as figure against a black background or the black *wa* is seen as figure against a white background. In the first two drawings in Group D, the figure-ground ambiguity is more conceptual in character. For these two drawings, I sacrificed the visual force of the competing interpretations to achieve some degree of self-reference (Drawing D1) or realization of the arch theme (Drawing D2). In such cases, one may consequently be able to experience both interpretations at once. In the remaining drawings in the group, though, the figure-ground reversals should prove to be more perceptually compelling.

D1 FIGURE IN GROUND

My attempt to render the six letters of the word Figure as figural patterns
against a ground formed by the six letters of the word Ground was not an
unqualified success. Nevertheless, the figure-ground ambiguity is quite strong
for the the first two letters of each of these words, thanks to a fortuitous complementarity of shape between the initial F of Figure and G of GROUND
and between the i of Figure and R of GROUND. Thus, the first letter tends
to be seen as F or G but not fully as both at once.[5]

D2 ARCH SUPPORT

In this more conceptual than perceptual figure-ground ambiguity, it is the open space in the wall that has the form of a typical arch. (Such an arch could thus find "support" within this space.)

D3 LES OBJETS D'ART SURRÉELS

This and the ensuing drawings of this group illustrate figure-ground ambigui-
ties that are more perceptually compelling than those in Drawings D1 and D2.
The two alternative perceptual interpretations may now be difficult to experi-
ence at the same time.

D4 BECKONING BALUSTERS

Here, on perceptual reversal, what was the ground becomes a row of figures in a more specific sense of the word figure. *(This drawing appeared on page 37 of the Winter 1984 issue of* The Stanford Magazine *and on page 104 of the April 1985 issue of* Smithsonian. *A life-sized row of three-dimensional columns of a similar design has recently been constructed by David Barker for display in San Francisco's science museum,* The Exploratorium.*)*

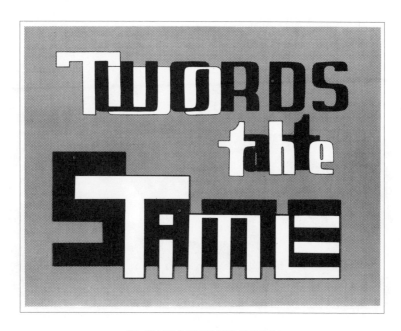

D5 SPACE-SAVING SUGGESTION

A decoding of the message is given in the Afterword.

D6 TIME-SAVING SUGGESTION

Rush-hour arrows—for getting down to business.

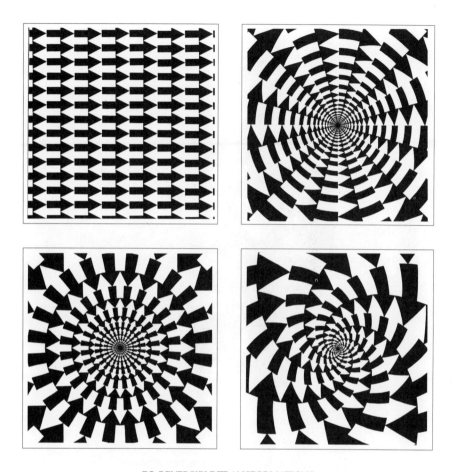

D7 REVERSIBLE TRANSFORMATIONS

The arrows in these four panels correspond to the uniform transformations of translation (upper left), rotation (upper right), dilation (lower left), and rotation plus dilation (lower right). The transformational reversibility in each case corresponds to the figure-ground reversibility of the black and the white arrows.

D8 SARA NADER

Two interpretations are made explicit in the Afterword.

D9 WRANGLING RUNGS

Do the white or the black bars constitute the rungs? Also, although they are, of course, uniformly white or black, do the upper halves of the white bars appear whiter than their lower halves? And do the lower halves of the black bars appear blacker than their upper halves?

E

FIGURE-GROUND IMPOSSIBILITIES

Each of the drawings in this group depicts what may at first glance appear to be something that could exist as a real object in the three-dimensional world. On closer examination, however, the "object" defies perceptual segregation, as a whole, from the nonobject or background and thus illustrates the strongest case of an "impossible object." Although the anomaly may be quickly evident in most of the drawings in this group, in some drawings the discovery of the anomaly may require careful scrutiny.

E1   L'EGS-ISTENTIAL QUANDARY

E2 ARC DE TRIPOD

(With apologies to the French.)

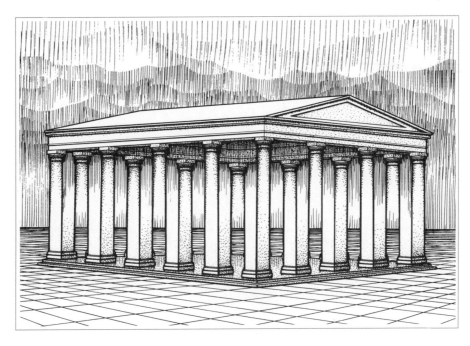

E3 DORIC DILEMMA

*(I also considered doing an analogous treatment of Colosseum columns
and giving it the title, Call 'em as you see 'em.)*

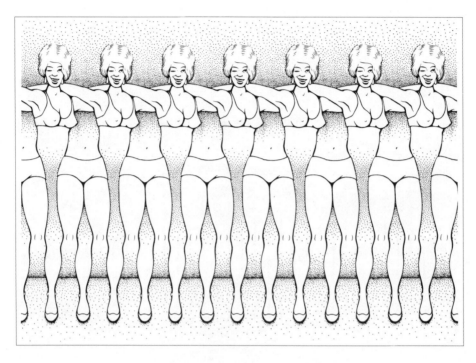

E4 CHORUS LINE CONUNDRUM TIME

"Now, left leg right, then right leg left. Right?"
*(Since this drawing was finished over 15 years ago, I have become sensitive
to objections that may legitimately be raised against the portrayal of women
presenting themselves as sex objects—let alone as anomalous objects. With
apologies, I am nevertheless including this drawing because the repeating pattern of the ambiguous figure-ground boundaries of the legs seems to induce a
particularly strong sense of visual restlessness.)*

JARRING SQUIRMS

E5 JARRING SQUIRMS

Globally consistent figure-ground segregation is not necessary for our recognition of letters—any more than for our recognition of people, animals, or buildings.

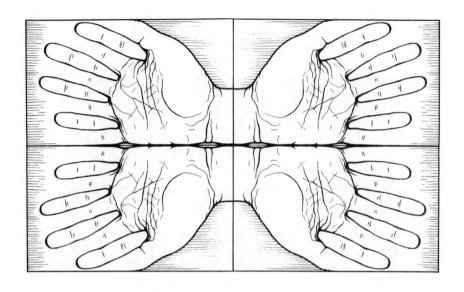

E6 EVEN, ODD, AND EVEN ODDER DIGITS

(Compliments to Michael Kubovy and Joseph Psotka, who came up with essentially this title for a scientific paper.[6])

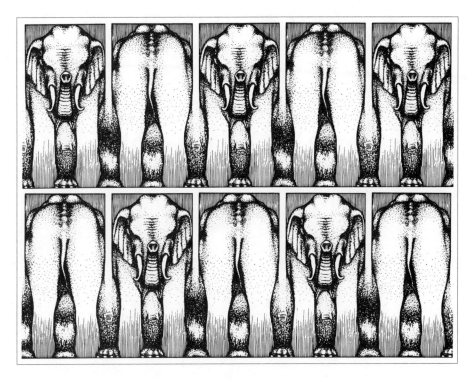

E7 PERIODIC STABLE OF THE ELEPHANTS

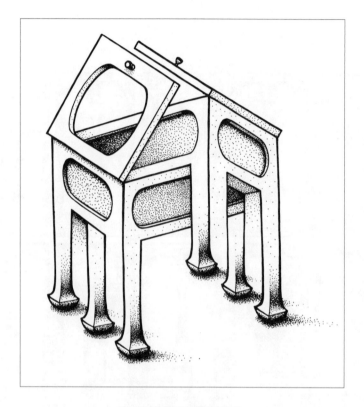

E8 CONVERSATION PIECE

My association to this drawing is a rule of conduct imposed in the dormitories of some women's colleges when I was an undergraduate in the 1940s: Although a woman and a male visitor may sit together on her bed while having a conversation, both parties must keep at least one foot on the floor at all times.

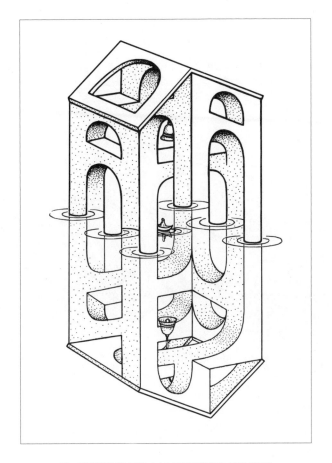

E9 CHECKING FOR A LEAK IN THE BASEMENT

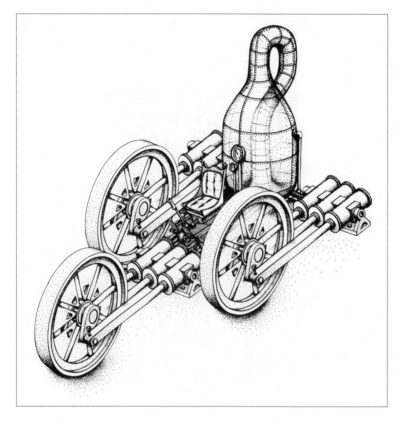

E10 STEAM-POWERED ANOMALOMOBILE

Can you find the anomalies in this drawing?

F

DEPTH IMPOSSIBILITIES

Strictly, the "impossible" objects included under this heading are highly improbable—not absolutely impossible. Each such object can be consistently segregated from the background and could actually exist as a three-dimensional object in space. To appear as it does in the drawing, however, the shape of the object would have to be very different from the shape that we normally expect for an object of the sort depicted. In addition, the object would have to be viewed from a very special vantage point of an "impossible object," an endless stairway like that at the top of the structure depicted here.[7]

F1 WROUGHT UP

F2 ARCH REMARK

The actual three-dimensional structure of this arch might be strangely twisted, or simply tipped back—so that the right-hand pedestal of the arch is suspended in the air (above the shadow indicated in the foreground). The apparently perfect alignment of this right-hand pedestal with the rectangular base in the background would then depend on the unlikely circumstance that we are viewing the scene from a very special vantage point.

F3 GRADUS AD PARNASSUM (À LA PENROSE & PENROSE)

(After L. S. Penrose and R. Penrose, who in 1958 introduced, as an example of an "impossible object," an endless stairway like that at the top of the structure depicted here.[7])

G

The anomalous aspects of the remaining drawings are more conceptual than perceptual. Still, the infinite regressions to which pictorial self-reference can lead have an arresting visual quality that must reflect something significant about the visual system. In most of the drawings in this group, the "infinite" regression is explicitly rendered—down, at least, to the limit of resolution permitted by the media of ink drawing, photo reduction, and/or unaided visual perception. In a few drawings, the infinite regression is only implied or suggested, as in *Scruting the Inscrutable* (Drawing G5), *Delicious Dear, But What's for Dessert?* (Drawing G7), and in a sense, *Gradus ad Parnassum* (Drawing F3) of the preceding group.

G1 LOOK AT MEEEEEE…

A familiar type of infinite regression—with an added twist.

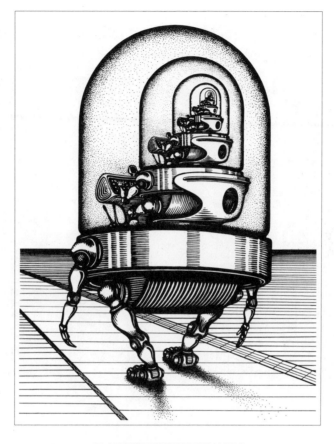

G2 I THINK, THEREFORE I AMBLE

Descartes, having concluded that the rest of the physical body is a machine operating according to strictly mechanical principles, proposed the pineal body of the brain as the seat of the soul. Concluding, from modern physiological evidence that the pineal body, like the body as a whole, operates according to strictly physical principles, I propose to put off to infinity the problem of the locus of the soul—as well as the problem of the locus of the eyes with which this hierarchical robot sees where it is going.

G3 HIERARCHY

Inspired by the Sierpinsky Carpet (in two dimensions) and the Menger Sponge (in three)—two fractal patterns named after the mathematicians who devised them.[8]

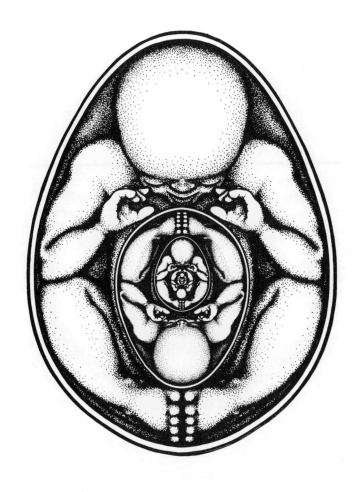

G4 EGGSPECTING

G5 SCRUTING THE INSCRUTABLE

Once after puzzling over why some words, like "scrutable," rarely occur without a qualifying prefix, such as the negating in-, I was moved to compose (and to publish[9]) the poem that appears on the facing page.

Plaint

O God, who art ept, you let
    us remain in-;
Our conceptions are maculate,
    Mary's was im-.

If we're kempt and we're couth
    for the nonce, we're soon un-,
Though our bent is, in truth,
    towards chalance more than non-.

Should affairs be complex,
    like the ill in the licit
Our faults become ex-
    that, until, were but plicit.

Awash as on oceans
    with ebrious helm,
The most effable notions
    may well underwhelm.

Yet we've reasons to peat,
    and to peat, and to re-,
As we watch our last feat
    slowly sink into de-:

Just as seasons flit past
    till they bring on the winters,
Our ludes never last
    half as long as the inters.

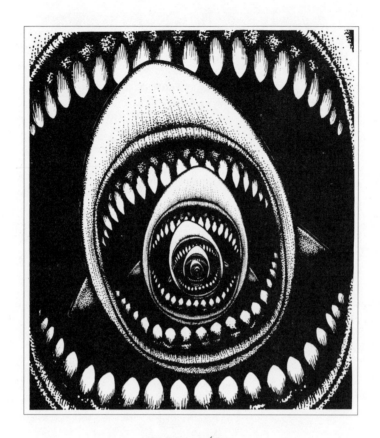

G6 BON APPÉTIT

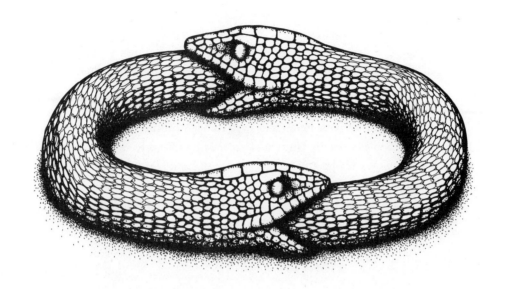

G7 DELICIOUS, DEAR, BUT WHAT'S FOR DESSERT?

H

Self-reference in a visual display becomes symbolic rather than pictorial when the display turns back on itself by naming or describing itself through conventional symbols such as letters or words, rather than by point-for-point iteration of itself through direct graphic duplication. Some of the drawings in the preceding groups have already made use of symbolic self-reference— for example, *Les Objets d'Art Surréels* (Drawing D3), *Space-Saving Suggestion* (Drawing D5), and *Jarring Squirms* (Drawing E5). Group H includes further examples in which symbolic self-reference is the principal feature.

H1 ARCH TYPE

Together and individually, the letters form the object they name.

H2 PLEASE SPELL US!

The title can be taken in two quite different ways—as a request by the four pictured individuals (1) for us to spell the word YOGA—either by simply naming its successive letters or by actually assuming bodily postures that form (from a suitable viewing position) those successive letters, and (2) for us to spell the four requestors themselves in the sense of taking their (very tiring) positions for them, so that they can rest. Indeed, spelling in both senses—of spelling the word and spelling the spellers—can here be achieved by one and the same act of bodily substitution.

H3 TROMPE-L'OEILÉPHANT FONT

Here, I have taken on the challenge of using purely black-and-white shading and shadows to attempt something approximating a trompe l'oeil—*an illusion in which the two-dimensional rendering of three-dimensional objects is so realistic that (under appropriate conditions) we might mistake the picture for the actual objects. (In the case of such an ink drawing, the "appropriate conditions" may include viewing it from a distance or, perhaps, through one eye.) This drawing, together with its title, harbors a potentially quadruple entendre. For, in French,* trompe *can be understood as the verb for "deceive"—as in* trompe l'oeil—*or it can be understood as the noun for an elephant's trunk—as in* trompe d'éléphant, *while the word* font *refers to a set of letters of a given graphic style (or, one might say, it refers to a type of type).*

H4 THE 5IVE 5ENSES

Here, I set myself the challenge of integrating into one picture, for each of the five senses (a) the verb appropriate to that sense (for example, see, for the sense of vision), (b) the noun for the organ of that sense (for example, eye), and (c) a graphic portrayal of that organ itself (for example, a picture of an eye). I gave myself license to depart from this constraint only for the fifth sense. For that, I incorporated the verb touch, *but instead of a noun for the organ of touch, I included the expletive that may follow too sharp a touch: "Ouch!" Also, in rendering the* o *of* ouch, *I portrayed the organ for emitting that expletive. The organ of the sense of touch is represented by the sharply "touched" finger—both in side view (as the top of the* T) *and in end view (as the dot of the exclamation point).*

TASTE

NOSE

SMELL

TOUCH!

endure
endure
enduce
chance
change

H5 ENDURE CHANGE

H6 TURN BACK

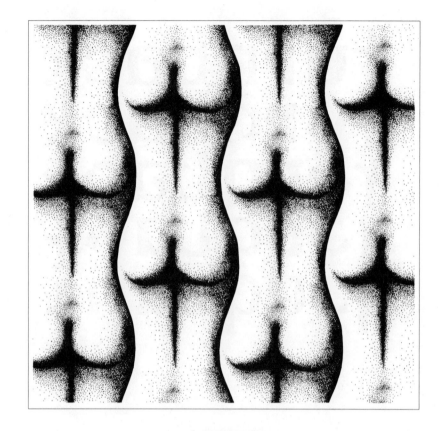

H7 ASSYMMETRY

H8 ARCHITEXTURE

H9 ALPHANUMERIC ESSENCES

Computer scientists attempting to design pattern recognition machines capable of recognizing a letter or number that may be written in countless different ways (for example, as **A**, **A**, A, ɑ, a, *or* *A*) *have asked such questions as: "What constitutes the 'A'-ness of the letter A?" From the drawings I have made in answer to such questions, I here include examples for two letters, V and O (to be pronounced "oh"), and the number, 10 (to be pronounced "ten").*

I

Under *transmogrifications* I include pictures that seem to portray objects that are at the same time familiar and grotesquely transformed. Pure transmogrifications are those that are not accompanied by another type of visual anomaly such as illusion, ambiguity, or impossibility. A transmogrification, while not sufficiently transformed to have lost the original meaning of the object transformed, may be sufficiently transformed toward some other object to pick up its meaning as well.

11 ARGH DE TROMP

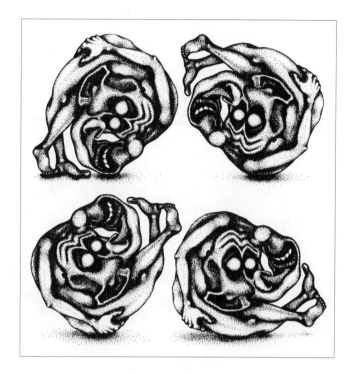

12 SOMERSAULT

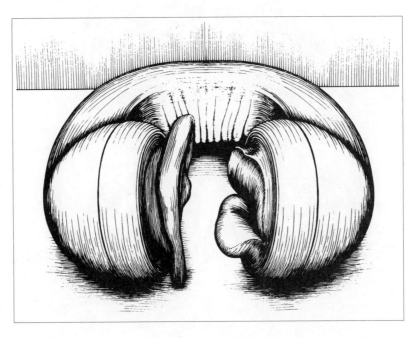

13 TELEPHONE CONFIDENCE

I4 METAMORPHOSIS

III

AFTERWORD

III

A F T E R W O R D

DRAWING FROM A BAG OF TRICKS

The drawings presented in Part II achieve their effects by means of various visual tricks. But to call them *tricks* is not to imply that they are without psychological significance. The tricks work by taking advantage of fundamental perceptual principles that have been shaped by natural selection in a three-dimensional world. Our ability to make pictures, which emerged only recently on an evolutionary time scale, enables us to present the eyes with visual patterns that systematically depart from the patterns that we and our ancestors experienced in nature. In considering the ways pictures can trick the eye, we can gain insight into the nature and ultimate source of the principles of visual perception.

Visual tricks could also be perpetrated without the use of two-dimensional pictures; however, for each visual trick attempted, we would have to undertake the fabrication of a whole three-dimensional scene. Moreover, we would have to confine each viewer of the scene to a single, fixed, monocular viewing point or peephole. To fool a visual system that has a full binocular and freely mobile view of a well-illuminated scene is next to impossible because, as the perceptual psychologist James Gibson emphasized, the optic information available to such a system is generally sufficient to specify the true spatial layout of the scene.[1] It is a testament to the effectiveness of natural selection in furnishing us with visual systems that make good use of this available information that our eyes almost never mislead us under well-illuminated natural viewing conditions.

A picture of a three-dimensional scene differs from the three-dimensional scene itself in a way that is crucial here. A picture not only represents that scene, it represents it as viewed from a particular position in space. The viewing position adopted by the artist who created the picture necessarily remains an inherent part of the depiction. Thereafter, this implicit viewing position determines how the picture is perceived. Moreover, it does so almost regardless of the location from which the picture itself is viewed—a position that differs from viewer to viewer, from moment to moment as the same viewer moves about, and even from the left to the right eye of a single stationary viewer. In effect, each picture of a three-dimensional scene carries with it its own built-in peephole. As a result, a picture can readily achieve anomalies—such as illusion, ambiguity, and impossibility—that are unlikely to arise in the three-dimensional world.

I turn now to a consideration of the visual tricks that I have used in my various drawings to produce illusion, ambiguity, impossibility, and other types of anomaly. My remarks are organized under headings corresponding to the nine categories into which the drawings themselves were grouped. I hope that my remarks, thus grouped, may serve as a preliminary taxonomy of visual tricks.

Depth Illusions

A visual stimulus becomes an illusion when normal observers consistently perceive some aspect of that stimulus in a way that differs from what can objectively be shown to be true of that aspect of the stimulus. Some illusions can be understood in terms of well-known principles of physical optics. Thus, because water and air have different indexes of refraction, a straight but slanting stick appears bent when half-immersed in water. Even a physical recording device will be subject to this illusion. For example, the illusory bend can be objectively measured in a photograph of the immersed stick. While such illusions are informative about the behavior of light, they do not tell us much that is specific to the human mind. Of greater psychological interest are illusions that are not already objectively present in the physical pattern of light reaching our eyes but that arise only in the psychological process of interpreting that pattern of light. In the variant of the Hering illusion incorporated in Drawing A6, *Gravitational Bending*, for example, the two portions of the apparently elliptical (or even circular) orbit that overlap the lines radiating from the central sun are curved only in the eye of the beholder. Objectively, these two horizontal portions of the "orbit" are perfectly straight, as can be verified by means of a ruler.

Although there are illusions of many kinds, the illusions illus-trated in my drawings depend primarily on our automatic tendency to impose a three-dimensional interpretation or depth organization on any visual array that could be the perspective projection of a three-dimensional object or scene. Figure III-1, which was inspired by a visual display devised by Dale Klopfer and Lynn Cooper for an experiment on apparent motion,[2] provides a convenient illustration. The perspective cues in this figure induce a depth interpretation in which the black dots A and B may appear to be closer to each other than either is to the dot C, and in which dot C may appear to be farther from dot A than from dot B. In fact, however, the centers of these three dots are exactly equi-distant from each other and so form an equilateral triangle in the plane of the picture.

My reasons for focusing on illusions deriving from depth interpre-tations are both practical and theoretical. From a practical standpoint, the medium of black-and-white ink drawings is well suited to the ma-nipulation of effective visual cues to depth—such as the cues known as *linear perspective*, *retinal size* (that is, the size of an image projected on the retina), and *occultation* (in which the view of a more distant object is partially blocked by a closer object along the same line of sight).[3] But this same medium is unsuited to the manipulation of the shades of lightness and color needed to demonstrate the different illusions of lightness or color contrast—in which, for example, a given surface appears lighter when preceded or surrounded by a contrastingly darker background, or appears redder when preceded or surrounded by a con-trastingly greener background. (Drawing D9, *Wrangling Rungs*, does

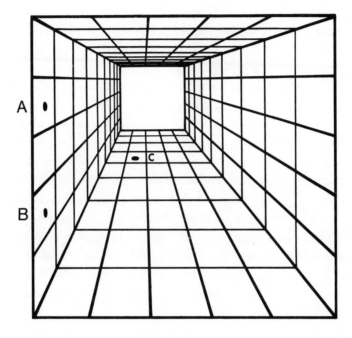

FIGURE III-1

A perspective illusion based on a visual display used by Dale Klopfer and Lynn Cooper to study apparent motion in depth. Despite appearances, the centers of the three black dots, A, B, and C, are equally distant from each other and form an equilateral triangle.

give rise to an illusion of lightness contrast; but it does so, evidently, as a result of figure-ground organization rather than as a result of manipulation of the actual color of the background.)

From a theoretical standpoint, illusions based on depth interpretation illustrate with special clarity how perceptual mechanisms that have evolved because they enabled our ancestors to function effectively in a three-dimensional world can lead us astray when we are required to make new sorts of judgments concerning new sorts of stimuli—such as two-dimensional pictures. Indeed, as has been argued, particularly by the British perception researcher Richard Gregory,[4] this tendency to impose a depth interpretation may explain many of the standard line-drawn visual illusions shown in psychology and perception textbooks (such as the Müller-Lyer, Poggendorff, Ponzo, and Zölner illusions, as well as the Hering illusion already discussed).[5]

Our perceptual machinery for making use of retinally available information about the disposition of objects in three-dimensional space is deeply entrenched in our nervous system and wholly automatic in its operation. Without our bidding or even our awareness of its existence, this machinery immediately goes to work on any visual input, including the visual input provided by a two-dimensional drawing. As a result, we cannot choose to see a drawing merely as what it is—a pattern of lines on a flat, two-dimensional surface. To the extent that that pattern of lines conforms with the rules of linear perspective, for example, that pattern automatically triggers the circuits in the brain that make the three-dimensional interpretation appropriate to such a perspective display. Any consciously adopted intentions to ignore such an interpretation are largely powerless against the swift deliverances of this underlying machinery. This should not surprise us. We have inherited this machinery from individuals who, long before the advent of picture making, interpreted—by virtue of this machinery—what was going on in the three-dimensional world around them with sufficient efficiency to survive and to continue our ancestral line.

In *Terror Subterra* (Drawing A1), the linear perspective of the subterranean tunnel (along with other depth cues, such as the relative heights of the projections of the two monsters on our retinas) supports the automatic perceptual inference that one of the two monsters is farther back in depth. The two monsters, nevertheless being exactly the same size in the drawing, subtend the same visual angle at the eye. The visual system therefore makes the additional inference that in order to subtend the same visual angle, the monster that is farther back in depth must also be larger.

Of course, other cues available to the visual system, such as binocular and motion parallax (as well as *accommodation*—the automatic adjustment of the lens of the eye to bring the image into sharp focus), provide counteracting evidence that the whole visual display is confined to a flat, two-dimensional surface and has no depth. These conflicting cues are not sufficient, however, to override the perspectively induced illusion of differences in depth and, hence, of size.

We remain oblivious to the anomalous character of many illusions until our visual experience is tested against some other, more objective evidence, such as that provided by measurement or tracing. There is nothing obviously amiss in *Turning the Tables* (Drawing A2) until one is told that the two seemingly differently shaped table tops are in fact identical in the picture plane. Clearly, this illusion arises because our visual system has once again given us depth interpretations of the two-dimensional drawing. The perspective cues indicate that the long axis of the table on the left goes back in depth while the long axis of the table on the right is more nearly at right angles to the line of sight. Now, if the table on the left goes back in depth, its retinal image must be correspondingly foreshortened. The fact that the retinal images of the two quadrilaterals interpreted as table tops are identical in length then implies that the real length of the table going back in depth must be greater than the real length of the crosswise table (and vice versa for their widths). Because the inferences about orientation, depth, and length are provided automatically by underlying neuronal machinery, any knowledge or understanding of the illusion we may gain at the intellectual level remains virtually powerless to diminish the magnitude of the illusion.

In the case of ambiguous figures, to be specifically considered in a moment, the anomaly may similarly escape our notice until the alternative perceptual interpretation of the figure is either called to our attention or spontaneously emerges in our perceptual experience. Unlike the visual illusions just considered, however, ambiguous figures yield alternative interpretations that can be experienced directly, without recourse to different, more objective operations. In particular, if the ambiguity is an ambiguity of depth interpretation, switches between the alternative interpretations can give rise to different illusions of size and shape of the sort just considered. Without having to make objective measurements, we can then simply see that the relative dimensions of parts of the drawing appear to change with each flip in perceptual interpretation.

Uncertain Circles (Drawing A3, also reproduced with labels in Figure III-2) illustrates this phenomenon. In one interpretation, we ignore the top parallelogram—C. Thereupon, we perceive the four parallelograms labeled A as the upper faces of four adjacent cubical blocks on the left (with the additional faces labeled D) and we perceive the two parallelograms labeled B as the upper faces of two adjacent rectangular blocks on the right (with the additional faces labeled E). The ellipses inscribed in the parallelograms labeled A, now seen as squares, come to be correspondingly seen as circles; and the ellipses inscribed in the parallelograms labeled B, now seen as elongated rectangles, come to be correspondingly seen as elongated ellipses. In the other interpretation, we take parallelogram C to be the top face of the upper of two vertically stacked larger cubical blocks and we ignore the parallelograms labeled D and E around the sides and bottom. Thereupon, the two ellipses inscribed in the parallelograms labeled B, now seen as the square faces of the large cubes, come to be seen correspondingly as circular; and the four ellipses inscribed in the parallelograms labeled A, now seen as the rectangular halves of such square faces, come to be seen correspondingly as flattened ellipses. In short, the circular or elliptical appearances of the very same closed curves reverse roles with each reversal of our depth interpretation of this ambiguous figure.

Incidentally, the complete object (including all the peripheral parallelograms—C, D, and E) is akin to the impossible objects to be

FIGURE III-2

A labeled verson of Drawing A3, Uncertain Circles. If the parallelogram and ellipse labeled C are ignored, the ellipses labeled A can be seen as circles in three-dimensional space while the ellipses labled B appear elongated vertically. If instead the parallelograms and ellipses D and E are ignored, the ellipses B can be seen as circles while the ellipses A appear elongated horizontally.

considered later. Each of the two favored interpretations is consistent with a subset of the parallelograms and ellipses—one interpretation with the subset A, B, D, and E, the other with the subset A, B, and C. But neither of these interpretations is compatible with the entire set of these parallelograms and ellipses.

Magician's Cabinet (Drawing A4) is similarly susceptible to two different depth interpretations, each yielding a different illusion of shape of a parallelogram and enclosed ellipse. If the right end of the cabinet is seen as a diagonal truncation of the box, the door that closes that end is seen as viewed from the outside and is seen as square with a circular window. If the right end of the cabinet is seen as at right angles to the cabinet, the door at that end is seen as viewed from the inside (as if the top and front of the cabinet had been removed) and is seen as rectangular with an elliptical window. This cabinet, too, is akin to the impossible objects in that while the former interpretation accords more completely with all the details of the drawing, the latter interpretation accords more completely with our usual expectations that the sides of boxes and cabinets are rectangular rather than trapezoidal and meet each other at right rather than at oblique angles.

Wrong-Way Arch (Drawing A5) carries a deviation from expectation to the point of blatant anomaly. What appears to be the outside of a strangely skewed and asymmetrical arch can be seen, by a reversal of perspective interpretation, as the inside of a quite normal, rectangular building. Purely by a mental act, we are able to achieve an architectural conversion from bizarre to traditional.

These illusions of depth, size, and shape depend on the use of the particular viewing position that is implied by the drawing. The two monsters of *Terror Subterra* have identical sizes in the picture only because the implied viewing position is so situated in space that the ratio of the distances of corresponding real monsters from that viewing position is equal to the ratio of the sizes of the monsters as they would exist in three-dimensional space. The designated rectangular surfaces portrayed in *Turning the Tables* project as identical parallelograms in the picture only because the implied viewing position has a particular location in space relative to the corresponding three-dimensional object. And a door diagonally affixed at the truncated end in *Magician's Cabinet* projects (in the picture or on the retina) as a parallelogram identical to that projected if the cabinet were rectangular only because the implied viewing position has been chosen precisely to achieve this congruence of projected shapes.

Depth Ambiguities

The examples just considered show how a picture constructed on the basis of a special vantage point can lead to alternative interpretations, each of which entails its own illusions. I now move on from the illusions that may result from such alternative interpretations to the ambiguity itself, and to the improbable alignments that underlie such ambiguities.

Open-and-Shut Case (Drawing B1) and *Rarebits of Adventure* (Drawing B2), which are variants of *Magician's Cabinet* (Drawing A4), provide for more than just two alternative interpretations. The various cues added in the different panels, by means of half-opened doors or inquisitive bunnies, favor quite different three-dimensional interpretations. As in *Magician's Cabinet*, each end of the basic box (as portrayed in the upper left panel of each illustration) can be seen as at right angles or as oblique to the box as a whole, and what is visible of that end door may appear to be either its outside or its inside surface. Moreover, the box (in addition to being seen as against a wall) can be seen either as resting on the floor or as suspended from the ceiling. The alternative interpretations are so numerous because the scene is portrayed as viewed from a very special vantage point in which, for example, each end of the box yields the same retinal projection whether that end is at right angles or oblique to the box as a whole.

The effect of a special viewing point is more dramatic in *Arch Rivals* (Drawing B3), reproduced with labels in Figure III-3. This, too, is a depiction of a three-dimensional structure that could actually be constructed in the world. The ambiguity that is the most arresting aspect of this picture would, however, be experienced only if the corresponding three-dimensional structure were viewed from the particular viewing point implied in the drawing. This is the unique viewing point yielding, in the viewer's retinal projection, an exact alignment between an outside edge (A or C in Figure III-3) of one arch and a similarly shaped inside edge of a second arch. Actually, such an alignment could be achieved in either of two situations that might exist in the world: (a) The arch inscribed *RIVALS* is smaller and closer to the viewer, in which case the surface B is the outside upper surface of that smaller arch; or (b) the arch inscribed *RIVALS* is behind the other arch, in which case the surface B is the inside undersurface of the other arch, inscribed *ARCH*.

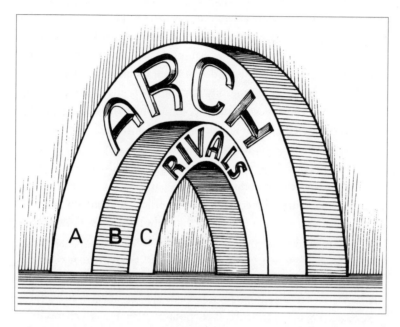

FIGURE III-3

A labeled version of Drawing B3. The curved surface B seems to share an edge both with the front surface, A, of the larger arch and with the front surface, C, of the smaller arch. Consequently, there is a rivalry between the incompatible interpretations of surface B as the lower surface of the larger arch and as the upper surface of the smaller arch.

Now, the probability that a freely mobile viewer will happen to view real objects in such a way that the projections of two different edges exactly coincide in this way is vanishingly small. The visual system therefore proceeds on the assumption that it is not viewing the world from such an unlikely viewing position. Accordingly, concerning the left edge of surface B, the visual system concludes that that edge is also the right edge of surface A of the arch inscribed ARCH. At the same time, concerning the right edge of surface B, the visual system concludes that that edge is also the left edge of surface C of the arch inscribed RIVALS. But the two conclusions are not simultaneously compatible with either of the two possible interpretations about the real dispositions of the two arches in space. The result is a continuing, unresolvable rivalry between the tendencies to see surface B as the underside of a larger arch and the upper side of a smaller arch.

Sister Rivals (Drawing B4) and *Egyptian-eyezed Tête-à-Tête* (Drawing B5) make similar use of an improbable alignment. The visual system, eschewing the hypothesis of an improbable alignment, at first tends to interpret *Sister Rivals* as a full-face view of one woman—even if she must appear peculiarly lopsided, cross-eyed, or mumpy. Also favoring the single, full-face interpretation (despite its accompanying distortion) are our greater experience in viewing faces frontally rather than in profile and, correspondingly, the presence in our brains of a greater number of neurons tuned to respond to full-face than to profile views.[6] Some additional inspection may therefore be needed before we see *Sister Rivals* as two normal faces—one, in profile view, in front of the right half of the other. In *Egyptian-eyezed Tête-à-Tête* the improbable alignment is between a face and a specially sculpted candlestick centered in front of the face. Owing to the coincidences between the contours of the candlestick and the features of the face, the single face may be seen, instead, as two mutually facing profiles, even though these must then appear as distorted and with eyes like those drawn by the ancient Egyptians. (In the latter interpretation, the tête-à-tête is between the two facing profiles; in the former interpretation, it is between the single face and the viewer.)

Reflecting Prince (Drawing B6) can be seen either as a frontal view of a strangely wide-faced (perhaps extraterrestrial) being or, alternatively, as a profile view of a normally proportioned human prince with his face (and hand) narcissistically pressed against a mirror. In the latter interpretation, though, the prince anomalously shares his nose with his reflection. Thus, in addition to illustrating ambiguity, this drawing also illustrates, to some extent, a variety of impossibility.

Object Ambiguities

The perceptual interpretation of a visual scene is determined not only by the point from which it is viewed. Its perceptual interpretation can also be affected by the orientation of the object with respect to the environment. A feature of the environment that has been particularly constant throughout evolutionary history is the upright direction conferred by the earth's gravitational field. We have accordingly come to use this highly reliable, environmentally determined upright direction to decide which is the intrinsic top of an object—a decision that is often crucial to our recognition of the identity of the object.[7] The variously rotated faces in *Glee Turns Glum* (Drawing C1) illustrate this phenomenon. Because we (and our ancestors) have usually viewed faces in their normal upright orientation, the face-recognizing circuits of our perceptual systems have become most sharply attuned or resonant to faces in this orientation.[8] Therefore, when we confront a stimulus that is especially contrived to appear facelike in either of two mutually inverted orientations, we tend to perceive the upright face and to overlook the upside-down face. Thus, although the faces are intrinsically identical in all three rows in *Glee Turns Glum*, we perceive glee across the top, turning across the middle, and glum across the bottom—and we continue to do so even when we turn the entire drawing upside down.

We are also accustomed to reading letters and numbers in their conventional upright orientations. Otherwise, letters such as M and W or *p*, *q*, *b*, and *d* would be quite ambiguous. Such potential ambiguities are brought out in the series of alphanumeric designs that follow *Glee Turns Glum*. In four of these (Drawings C2, C3, C5, and C6) a given alphanumeric character plays different roles depending on the orientation of its context. Thus, in *One To Three* (Drawing C2) the *w* of *Two* is also the *E* in *ONE* and the *3* in *0123*, and in *Zen and the Art of Cycle Maintenance* (Drawing C6), a given character is interpreted as both the *Z* and the *N* of *ZEN*.

More challenging is *Conveyor Error Horror* (Drawing C7), in which all the letters making up a sentence are identical in intrinsic shape and are distinguished only by the positions in which that shape is placed. (For those who have not deciphered the resulting message, it is "A jagged edge pegged padded baggage agape.")

Finally, *Four In Five* (Drawing C4) differs from the other members of this series in that the ambiguity that it illustrates (an ambiguity of *IV*) depends not on the orientation of the context but on the form of the context—namely, whether that context is composed of Roman letters or of Roman numerals.

Figure-Ground Ambiguities

Nothing more needs to be said here about the first two ambiguities in this group, *Figure in Ground* (Drawing D1) and *Arch Support* (Drawing D2, in which the arch is conspicuous in its absence). As I have noted, these two ambiguities must be deemed more conceptual than perceptual. It is the remaining figure-ground ambiguities in this group that are of greatest perceptual interest.

Les Objets d'Art Surréels (Drawing D3) and *Beckoning Balusters* (Drawing D4) both make use of three-dimensional modeling and symmetry to heighten the conflict between the two alternative interpretations. In the ensuing drawings, the complementarity between the black and the white areas is used to achieve the same effect. For those who did not completely unpack the message in *Space-Saving Suggestion* (Drawing D5), it is: "Two words at the same time." The following *Time-Saving Suggestion* (Drawing D6) speaks, I think, for itself—as does the set called *Reversible Transformations* (Drawing D7). (The latter correlates reversal of motion with complementation of color—that is, reversal of black and white. It also illustrates some of the motions that we find to be psychologically simplest or most natural in laboratory studies using real, apparent, and imagined motions.[9] As I suggest later, the possibilities of these spatial transformations, having become deeply internalized in our visual systems, may underlie our predispositions both to appreciate the symmetrical patterns to which such transformations give rise and also to spontaneously experience such patterns in certain circumstances or states.[10])

Sara Nader (Drawing D8) exemplifies a somewhat different kind of ambiguity in which the two alternative figures are not strictly complementary. While the black area constitutes the figure in one interpretation, the white and black areas together constitute the figure in the other interpretation (with the black areas then corresponding to dark or shadowed portions of the figure). For those who have not yet been successful in experiencing both perceptual interpretations of *Sara Nader*, Figure III-4 introduces additional cues to bring out each interpretation in turn. On the left, we have the windblown serenader with his saxophone (and a little bird on the wing). On the right, we have the presumed object of the saxophonist's musical effort, Sara Nader herself. (Is it not interesting, by the way, that a face that is delineated as sketchily as the Sara Nader of the original Figure III-5 can still be seen as attractive?)

In connection with *Glee Turns Glum* (Drawing C1), I mentioned that we are particularly discriminating of faces in their normal upright orientation. Figure III-5 illustrates this for Sara Nader. In the inverted portrait, she is more difficult to see, and surely, her attractiveness is more difficult to assess. The same appears to be true following complementation (reversal of white and black) and, of course, following the combination of inversion and complementation. In contrast, the cari-

FIGURE III-4

The two alternative interpretations of the ambiguous Drawing D8,
Sara Nader, *rendered explicit.*

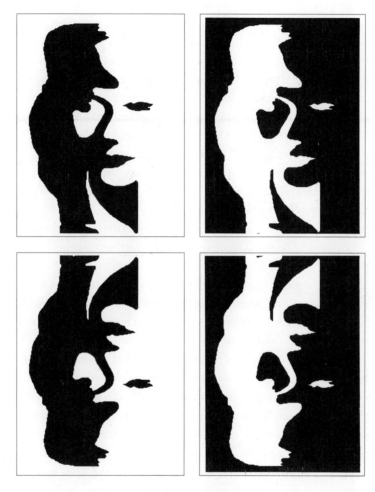

FIGURE III-5

The original ambiguous drawing Sara Nader (upper left), and three variants—obtained by inversion (turning upside down), by complementation (reversing black and white), and by a combination of inversion and complementation. Does the silhouette caricature of the saxophonist retain its recognizability better than the face of Sara Nader herself after these transformations?

cature of the saxophonist appears to suffer much less perceptual degradation under inversion or complementation. In part, this may be because appreciation of the caricatured silhouette does not require discrimination of the subtle nuances of facial expression or attractiveness that become inaccessible to us under inversion. In part this may also be because we have learned to recognize objects in silhouette form, both as dark figures against a bright sky and as brightly illuminated figures against a deeply shaded background. Natural scenes have not provided us with much occasion to recognize three-dimensional objects under reversed shading in which, for example, concave, lower, and hence, normally shadowed areas of the face are lighter and convex, upper, and, hence, normally illuminated areas of the face are darker.

Wrangling Rungs (Drawing D9) rings further changes on the theme of black-and-white reversible figures. Notice that in the upper half, it is the white vertical bands that seem to constitute the figural rungs of the railing, while in the lower half, it is the black vertical bands. Why is this? The reason, I suggest, is that bilaterally symmetrical shapes tend to be perceived as figure. Only the upper halves of the white bands are symmetrical, while only the lower halves of the black bands are symmetrical. This may be yet another manifestation of the visual system's assumption that it is not viewing the world from a special vantage point. While the two sides of the same face, animal, fruit, or human artifact are often mutually symmetrical, the contours of separate objects are rarely mutually symmetrical—unless they are carefully positioned and viewed from a special vantage point. Hence, if two contours in nature yield symmetrical retinal projections, they probably belong to the same object and, as such, should be interpreted as figure. If the spaces intervening between such a figure and the next are asymmetrical, this only reinforces such a figure-ground segregation. Although a visual system operating on this principle evidently serves us well in natural settings, it is apt to be confounded by a contrived display such as *Wrangling Rungs*, in which one half of the display dictates one parsing into figure and ground while the other half dictates the complementary parsing. Because such a visual dilemma does not admit a global resolution, it is like the impossible objects to which I turn next.

Before leaving *Wrangling Rungs*, however, I note one other, quite remarkable phenomenon. Although actually uniform in their colors, the white bars appear whiter at their symmetrical tops, and the black bars appear blacker at their symmetrical bottoms. Perhaps the perceptual interpretation of a region as figure confers on that region an enhanced visual salience in the form of an apparent intensification of its distinguishing color.[11]

Figure-Ground Impossibilities

The elephant in *L'egs-istential Quandary* (Drawing E1) belongs to a class of objects that are truly impossible in that the object itself cannot be globally segregated from the nonobject or background. Parts of the object (in this case the elephant's legs) become the background, and vice versa. My archetypal example of figure-ground impossibility is *Arc de Tripod* (Drawing E2), which is a minor variant of that early, simplest, and perhaps most widely familiar impossible object—the two-branched trident. My impossible Greek temple, *Doric Dilemma* (Draw-

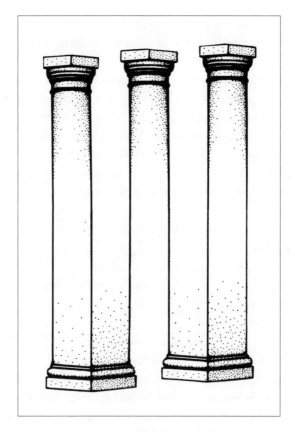

FIGURE III-6

Some adjacent columns from Drawing E3, Doric Dilemma. The fiure-ground anomaly and its correspondence to that of the well-known impossible two-pronged trident become more obvious when just these (two square or three circular) columns are shown.

ing E3), is an elaboration of this same idea. Closer examination of a columnar component (Figure III-6) shows this (and the appropriateness of an alternative title: *Squaring the Circle*).

Each of the drawings in Group E is similarly based on the impossibility of consistently parsing the whole picture into figure and ground. *Jarring Squirms* (Drawing E5) shows that letters can be impossible objects—without, however, being impossible to read. My *Steam-Powered Anomalomobile* (Drawing E10) illustrates the point that an impossible object can become so complex, however, that the visual system fails to register the local figure-ground inconsistencies. We then experience a global object that, however unconventional, may appear perfectly possible. Only detailed scrutiny will then reveal the local anomalies, and even after having found them, we may still revert to our visual impression of the soundness of the object as a whole. Beyond the conceptual, if not perceptual, anomaly of the steam boiler having the form of Klein's bottle (a one-sided closed surface conceived by the mathematician Felix Klein), there are two design flaws that render this conveyance not just impractical but impossible: The piston rods are variants of the original two-branched trident, and the spokes of the wheel similarly shift figure-ground status between hub and rim.

Depth Impossibilities

The big wheel *Wrought Up* (Drawing F1) presents in its stark simplicity a much more visually compelling mechanical anomaly. Yet, it belongs to a class of impossible objects that, as I have noted, are not so strictly impossible. There is no fundamental unparsability, here, into object and nonobject or into figure and ground. The picture could be of an actual three-dimensional object. Thus, an iron wheel could be cast with a highly warped form such that—from just this special vantage point—the oddly twisted spokes of the wheel project as straight lines resembling those of a normal cast iron wheel. What we have here is not strictly impossibility but a double improbability—the improbability of an object being twisted in just such a way that it yields a projection resembling that of a normal, nontwisted object; and the improbability of viewing it from exactly the position that yields that misleading projection. Under natural conditions, such a double improbability may qualify as a virtual impossibility.

The drawing *Arch Remark*: "I Stand Corrected" (Drawing F2) could similarly be considered the depiction of an actual three-dimensional structure. Like the wheel, it might have a strangely twisted shape that is viewed from the unique vantage point at which the twisted edges still project as straight lines. Or, as I noted in my remarks accompanying the drawing, the three-dimensional structure might simply be tipped back so that the right-hand pedestal is suspended in the air in the foreground and so that from the specially chosen vantage point, that pedestal appears to be perfectly aligned with the rectangular base of the arch in the background.

Gradus ad Parnassum (Drawing F3) is an elaboration of one of several ingenious drawings put forward as "impossible objects" in a psychological article by a British geneticist father, L. S. Penrose, and theoretical physicist son, Roger Penrose.[12] In another variant, this anomalous stairway has also been featured in a well-known etching by the Dutch graphic artist M. C. Escher.[13] I originally prepared my version of these "steps to perfection" to serve as a visual accompaniment for my auditory illusion of an endlessly rising tone.[14] I include the drawing here as another example of a three-dimensional structure that, while possible, appears impossible from the chosen viewing position. The actual structure might be a nonanomalous staircase that spirals up to a topmost step (labeled A, in the simplified view shown in Figure III-7). In the real staircase, this top step would be both higher and closer to the viewer than the apparently adjacent back-corner step (labeled B). If we could shift this viewing point just a bit to the left, we would immediately see that these two steps are not adjacent and that a chasm yawns between the topmost step, A, and the much lower and farther back step, B.

Anomalies based on depth organization and figure-ground organization are closely related. The portion of a picture that is perceived as figure is also perceived to be in front of the portion that is perceptually relegated to the role of background. A perceptual reversal of figure and ground therefore entails a reversal in perceived depth. Similarly, an object that is impossible because it cannot be globally parsed into figure and ground is also one that cannot be globally structured in depth. (The opposite is not necessarily true, however. The anomalies in some of the drawings, such as in the "archetypal" anomaly *Arch Remark* [Drawing F2], depend on an ambiguity or incompatibility of depth but not, as in the "archetypal" anomaly *Arc de Tripod* [Drawing E2], of figure and ground.)

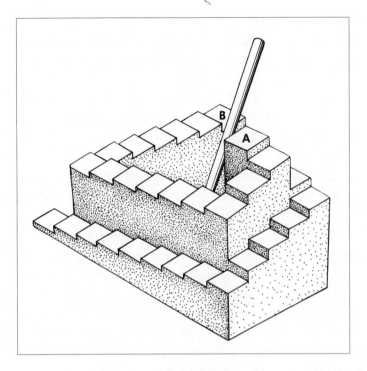

FIGURE III-7

The apparently endless top flight of the stairway in Drawing F3, Gradus ad
Parnassum *(à la Penrose & Penrose). In three-dimensional space the stairway itself need not be anomalous. Step B could be lower and farther back than
step A, with a yawning gap between these two steps. The anomalous appearance arises only from the particular viewing point built into the picture, which
ensures that the retinal projection of step B is so aligned with the retinal projection of step A as to give the appearance that B is the next step up from A.*

Pictorial Self-Reference

The anomalous aspects of the remaining drawings are more conceptual than perceptual. Still, infinite regressions, considered in this section, also have an arresting visual quality that must surely reflect something significant about the visual system.

I had my own first encounter with infinity when, as a child, I visited a barber shop with large mirrors on opposite walls. Since that time, I have come across many an illustration, cartoon, magazine cover, or advertisement that includes a portrayal of itself and, hence, a portrayal of a portrayal of itself, ad infinitum. In confronting us with the question, "Where does it all end?" such pictures can stir up some of our deepest conceptual perplexities about space and time, about beginnings and endings. The geometrically regular repetitions and symmetries inherent in a picture—such as *Look at Meeeeee . . .* (Drawing G1)—that is a picture of the picture of the picture, ad infinitum, also have a direct visual appeal. This visual appeal may exist for the same reason that similar geometrically regular patterns—including, in particular, such "form constants" as tunnels and spirals[15]—are spontaneously experienced when the visual circuits of the brain have been rendered irritable by drugs, fever, sleep deprivation, flashing light, or the like. Symmetries and regularities arise from iterated application of spatial transformations of the types that both evolutionary considerations and perceptual experiments indicate must be deeply entrenched in the brain.

HierArchy (Drawing G3) illustrates a related kind of symmetry known as *scale invariance*, in which greater and greater magnification reveals only the same pattern, repeated without limit on smaller and smaller scales. Such patterns belong to a subspecies of fractal patterns, which are currently of considerable mathematical interest—and sometimes of great visual beauty.[16] The infinite regression is not explicitly depicted but only implied in two of the drawings in this group—namely, in the exercise in sick humor, *Delicious, Dear, But What's for Dessert?* and in *Scruting the Inscrutable*, where the regression becomes trapped in a cycle of self-referential play between eyes and lips.

Symbolic Self-Reference

A picture portraying itself, a robot controlling itself, a mirror reflecting a second mirror that is reflecting the first (and hence reflecting itself), and a snake swallowing a second snake that is swallowing the first (and hence swallowing itself) all entail some kind of recursive self-reference. It is but a short step to the symbolic self-reference exemplified by a word or letter that in some way refers back to itself, or graphically instantiates the thing it names (in a kind of visual analogue of onomatopoeia). Several of the drawings already presented, as illustrations of other anomalies, have also exemplified symbolic self-reference. In *Les Objects d'Art Surréels* (Drawing D3), the spaces between the surreal objects had the shapes of the successive letters of the word *spaces*. In *Space-Saving Suggestion* (Drawing D5), the two words *Same* and *Time* were conjoined, as figure and ground and, hence, could only exist at the same time. And, in *Jarring Squirms* (Drawing E5), the shapes of the impossible letters were jaggedly angular and, hence, jarring for the word *JARRING* and twistingly wormlike and, hence, squirmy for the word *SQUIRMS*. The word that provides symbolic self-reference back to the picture may also be only implied or suggested by the picture, rather than explicitly contained in it. Thus, there is a kind of symbolic self-reference in *Beckoning Balusters* (Drawing D4) when, on perceptual reversal, what was the ground becomes a row of figures, in a more concrete and specific sense of the word *figure*.

Self-reference is more obvious in the first few drawings of Group H, including *Please Spell Us!*, *Trompe-l'oeiléphant Font*, and *The 5ive 5enses* (Drawings H2, H3, and H4). In *Endure Change* and *Turnback* (Drawings H5 and H6), however, self-reference depends on visually implied processes of transformation. Thus, through continuous deformation of its component letters, the word *endure* endures a change into *change*. (Moreover, it endures this change through *chance*.) Intermediate stages provide further illustrations of object ambiguity. The ambiguity is not of the semantic type most common for words (in which, for example, *change* could mean either an alteration or some coins) but of a visual type—in which, for example, the first three letters of the word could be either *end* or *cha*.

Transmogrifications

I reserve the category of transmogrifications primarily for pictures in which an interpretation-altering transformation is portrayed or implied that is different from the simple geometric transformations that I have already mentioned. So far, I have discussed only uniform translations (for example, rigid shifts left or right, or up or down), rotations, reflections, changes in size, or combinations of these. And, in fact, the transformations that have repeatedly emerged in all the preceding categories have mostly been of these simple geometric types. Thus:

—*Under Illusions (Group A)*, we have *Terror Subterra* (Drawing A1), in which the two monsters differed by a translation and (seemingly) a size change; and *Turning the Tables* (Drawing A2), in which the implied rotation between the table tops seemed nonrigid (that is, not only translated and rotated but also stretched in length relative to width). In both cases, of course, the transformation in the plane of the picture itself, however, was carried out rigidly, without stretching.

—*Under Depth Ambiguities (Group B)*, we have *Open-and-Shut Case* (Drawing B1), in which the various alternative disambiguations were achieved by implied rigid rotations of the cabinet doors in three-dimensional space; and perhaps *Sister Rivals* and *Reflecting Prince* (Drawings B4 and B6), in which the perception of two normal facial images (rather than one distorted full-face image) may depend on the viewer imagining (however implicitly or unconsciously) a 90° rotation or 180° reflection, respectively, of one of the two faces into the other.

—*Under Object Ambiguities (Group C)*, we have *Glee Turns Glum*, *Zen and the Art of Cycle Maintenance*, *Conveyor Error Horror* (Drawings C1, C6, and C7), and several of the other alphanumeric ambiguities (Drawings C2, C3, and C5), in which an implied rotation changes the interpretation of a face, letter, number, or other object.

—*Under Figure-Ground Ambiguities (Group D)*, we have *Beckoning Balusters* (Drawing D4) and *Time-Saving Suggestion* (Drawing D6, with the "rush hour arrows"), in which the figural objects (stone balusters or hurriedly descending commuters) are separated by spaces that (in addition to being shaped as human figures or as arrows) differ from each other only by translations and reflections; and *Reversible Transformations* (Drawing D7), in which all uniform transformations in the plane—translation, rotation, size scaling, and a combination of these—are explicitly represented in the complementary and reverse-directed arrows of reversible figure and ground.

—*Under Figure-Ground Impossibilities (Group E)*, we have, in addition to reflections (as in Drawings E6 and E9), the recurrent theme of repeating elements that vie with each other for the status of figure, as opposed to ground—namely, legs in *L'egs-istential Quandary*, *Chorus Line Conundrum Time*, *Periodic Stable of the Elephants*, and *Conversation Piece* (Drawings E1, E4, E7, and E8); columns in *Doric Dilemma* (Drawing E3); upright bars of letters in *Jarring Squirms* (Drawing E5), and fingers in *Even, Odd, and Even Odder Digits* (Drawing E6). Such repeating elements are related to each other by translations.

—*Under Depth Impossibilities (Group F)*, we have *Wrought Up* (Drawing F1), in which the repeating elements (spokes of the wheel) are related to each other by rotation rather than translation; and *Gradus ad Parnassum* (Drawing F3), in which the repeating elements (steps of the stairway) ascend in approximation to a converging spiral. A spiral, incidentally, arises from a combination of a rotation and either a change of scale or, as the spiral is approximated here, a (vertical) translation.

—*Under Pictorial Self-References (Group G)*, we have the recurrent theme of repeating elements but, this time, elements that are related primarily by changes in size (as in Drawings G1 through G6). The size scaling, rather than being essentially the only transformation, as in

I Think, Therefore I Amble (Drawing G2) or *Bon Appétit* (Drawing G6), may, however, be combined with other uniform transformations, such as rotations, as in *Look at Meeeeee…*(Drawing G1) and (without explicit size scaling) in *Delicious, Dear, But What's for Dessert?* (Drawing G7), translations, as in *HierArchy* (Drawing G3), and reflections, as in *Eggspecting* (Drawing G4).

—*And, under Symbolic Self-References (Group H)*, we have repeating elements that often differ from each other, in part, by a translation—from left to right, as in the successive letters of the words in *Please Spell Us!* and *Trompe-l'oeiléphant Font* (Drawings H2 and H3), or from top to bottom, as in the successive transformations of the words in *Endure Change* or *Turnback* (Drawings H5 and H6). And *Assymmetry* and *Architexture* (Drawings H7 and H8), which qualify for inclusion under symbolic self-reference only when taken together with the accompanying "texts" of their titles, contain pictorial elements that are related purely by translations.

In this last category (that of symbolic self-reference), however, the elements generally do differ by some additional, and not purely geometric, structure- or texture-altering transformation between the successive, similar-appearing elements (bodily postures, elephant trunks, letters, or other objects).

Beyond simple geometric transformations, there are pictorial deformations of infinite variety that can take an object into countless intrinsically different forms, each of which may represent or resemble something quite different from the original object—or nothing at all. Indeed, the most radical of implied visual transformations may be those in which something (figure or object) is transformed into nothingness (ground or nonobject), as in the figure-ground impossibilities (Group E). Thus, one might say that the legs of the elephant in *L'egs-istential Quandary* (Drawing E1) transform into nonexistents and vice versa.

The principal criterion that I have used for classifying drawings in this last group—transmogrifications—is that they seem to portray objects that are at the same time familiar and grotesquely transformed. Many of the drawings already classified under other headings tend to give an initial impression of this kind. Thus, *Wrong-Way Arch, Sister Rivals, Wrought Up*, and *Arch Remark* (Drawings A5, B4, F1, and F2) all tend to be perceived as strangely distorted, warped, or twisted variants of some familiar object such as an archway, face, or wheel.

As an "archetypal" example of transmogrification, however, I offer *Argh de Tromp* (Drawing I1), which represents this type of anomaly without the complications of visual illusion, ambiguity, or object impossibility. In *Somersault* (Drawing I2), I combined an explicitly presented rigid transformation (rotation) with an implicitly suggested transmogrification, in which a human figure (especially its face) is twisted up into a contorted, vortical caricature of itself, rolling over and over. The nonrigid transformation need not merely be away from a familiar object. As in *Argh de Tromp* (Drawing I1) and in the letters in *Endure Change* and *Turnback* (Drawings H5 and H6), it can also be toward some other object or objects. *Telephone Confidence* and *Metamorphosis* (Drawings I3 and I4) are further examples.

Artists or many styles have long explored anomalies of transmogrification. The results of such explorations include the variously elongated faces and figures by El Greco, Amedeo Modigliani, and Alberto Giacometti; the limp watches and stilt-legged elephants by Salvador Dali; the scrambled features and figures by Pablo Picasso; the contorted bodies by Francis Bacon; and the soft sculptures of household appliances by Claes Oldenburg, to mention just a few.

I suggest that our responses to such works depend both on the objects that have been transformed and on the transformations themselves. On one hand, if the original object is totally unfamiliar and uninterpretable, or if the transformation applied to that object is too extreme, the result becomes a purely abstract design. It may possess visually appealing symmetries and colors, but its ability to engage the internal schemas, archetypes, or feelings that have come to be elicited by significant real objects during our evolutionary history is severely limited. On the other hand, if the original object is wholly ordinary and if the transformation applied to that original object is negligible or nonexistent, the result, like a run-of-the-mill photograph, provides us with no significant new experience. The scene or object may readily be recognized, but it is also banal.

More challenging to our perceptual/cognitive system is the case of a meaningful object that has been transformed to just such a degree that we still recognize the original object in the transformed result and simultaneously recognize that the result is no longer that familiar object. We are thus made aware of potentialities that resided in the original object all along. And a depiction of one meaningful object transformed into another meaningful object may become doubly meaningful.

The effects that such transformed objects have on us are not unlike our perceptual shock on encountering an old friend whose appearance has been altered by age, accident, or disease; or our wonder on seeing a young person of (formerly) indifferent appearance and dress coming down the aisle in white lace as a radiantly beautiful bride; or our fascination with the resemblance between the appearances of a close friend and what we detect in a photograph of that person as a child or in a photograph of a parent of that person.

Having considered some of the specific visual tricks illustrated by the drawings, I turn now to a broader consideration of what such tricks reveal about perception, about the perception of pictures, and about the human mind.

PERCEPTION, PICTURES, ANOMALIES, AND THE MIND

What we see is a reflection not only of what is out there in the world. What we see is also a reflection of what our own minds bring to the act of perceiving. This is illustrated by the slight delay we may experience in recognizing the voice or face of someone we well know, when we unexpectedly encounter that voice or face in a totally new context. More dramatically, it is illustrated by the failures of individuals, mentioned in my autobiographical note in the Foreword, to recognize a peeled hard-boiled egg when expecting to feel a firm gear-shift knob, to recognize hot syrup when expecting to taste unsweetened coffee, or to recognize one's own reflection when expecting to see an unoccupied room. Individuals with damage to certain parts of the brain, who fail to recognize even their everyday surroundings or closest friends and relatives, may repeatedly be subject to similar catastrophic reactions.

Through my drawings, I have tried to show that the role of mental interpretation also emerges—and with a special kind of clarity—in our perception of pictures. Objectively, a drawing is only an array of marks on a two-dimensional surface. Yet, on viewing such a surface, we may in a definite sense see a three-dimensional scene populated with solid objects—people, animals, furniture, rooms, buildings, and the like. The sense in which we "see" a three-dimensional scene in a flat drawing is, however, a curious one that can best be brought out by first considering an extreme form of art in which the eye is fooled into a more literal kind of seeing.

Trompe l'oeil

A painting of the special type known as *trompe l'oeil* (literally, "deceive the eye") is one that has been so executed and so presented to our view that the optical images that are projected onto the retinas of our eyes do not differ from the optical images that would be projected if the painting were replaced by an actual three-dimensional scene corresponding to the (real or imagined) one depicted in the painting. From previous centuries, the most numerous examples of trompe l'oeil are the small paintings of arrays of flat objects—old letters, photographs, and other mementos—realistically painted, with their creases, faded colors, tattered edges, and shadows, as if these items were actually tacked on a bulletin board or stuck in the edges of a framed picture.

The single most ambitious trompe l'oeil may be the fresco covering the ceiling of the Church of Sant'Ignazio in Rome (Figure III-8). Fra Andrea Pozzo painted this ceiling to simulate an open, skyward extension of the church itself, with Sant'Ignazio, surrounded by a host of angels and cherubim, ascending into heaven.[17] Modern examples of trompe l'oeil include the large murals—of windows, doors, people, entire other buildings, or outdoor scenes—sometimes painted with deceptive realism on the otherwise blank sides of city buildings.

The one drawing in which I have tried, within the severe constraints inherent in the medium of pen and ink, to achieve a trompe-l'oeil effect, is the anomaly of symbolic self-reference that I called *Trompe-l'oeiléphant Font* (Drawing H3). A true deception would require, instead, a large, full-color photograph of high definition or a painting of meticulously photographic realism and special viewing

FIGURE III-8

Photograph of the Pozzo ceiling. (From Scala / Art Resource.)

conditions. The following list sets forth the most essential of these viewing conditions. (For more complete, and highly illuminating, accounts of trompe l'oeil, see Maurice Henri Pirenne's *Optics, Painting, and Photography*[18] and Michael Kubovy's *The Psychology of Perspective and Renaissance Art.*[19])

1. We should be far enough from the painting that we can not visually resolve the textural features of the painted surface itself—features that would furnish cues to the flat, two-dimensional character of that surface. (Such textural features might include individual paint dabs, brush marks, dust particles, or the warp and weft of the canvas.)

2. We should be far enough from the painting, relative to the distance between our two eyes, that there is negligible difference in the images projected on our two retinas as a consequence of binocular parallax. (See Figure III-9a.) Or, alternatively, we should view the painting *monocularly*, that is, through one eye only—perhaps, perforce, through a single peephole provided for the purpose. (Small trompe-l'oeil paintings, which cannot be seen well from a distance, typically minimize the role of binocular parallax by portraying only relatively flat objects mounted on a flat surface—thus ensuring virtually identical retinal images even under relatively close viewing.)

3. We should remain sufficiently stationary that there is negligible difference in the images projected even on the same retina at different times as a consequence of motion parallax. (Again, see Figure III-9a.) Such a stationary view might also be ensured by a fixed peephole.

4. Our viewing position (or the location of the peephole) should be at the approximate distance and direction from the painting for which

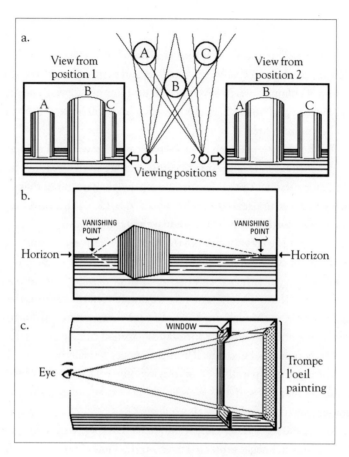

FIGURE III-9

(a) An illustration of two cues to depth: binocular parallax, in which the views of the world obtained from the viewpoints of the left and right eyes differ and, hence, provide information about the disposition of objects in space; and occultation, in which a nearer object (cylinder B) cuts off the view of different portions of more distant objects (cylinders A and C), depending on the viewpoint. (b) A schematization of another depth cue, linear perspective, in which parallel lines in space converge to a vanishing point in the picture; the vanishing point is on the horizon line if the parallel lines are horizontal in space. (c) Viewing conditions conducive to a trompe-l'oeil effect.

the perspective of the painting was designed. For example, our viewing position should be at the height of any vanishing points for lines that would be horizontal in the three-dimensional scene or, equivalently, at the height of any explicitly painted horizon line. (See Figure III-9b.)

5. The painting should be situated behind a window, door, or other opening, so that while the painted surface remains uniformly illuminated, its edges (which would otherwise provide a clue to the flat, rectangular character of its physical surface) are, from our vantage point, hidden from view. (See Figure III-9c.)

6. The rendering of highlights and shadows in the painting (the chiaroscuro) should be consistent with the illumination that actually prevails in the viewing space (called the *ambient* illumination). In particular, if the prevailing illumination comes primarily from above (as it usually has in our own experience, as well as in that of our ancestors), regions representing convex objects in the painting should be rendered with their upper portions lighter and their lower portions darker and, as in *Trompe-l'oeiléphant Font* (Drawing H3), with the rendering of the shadows appropriately lower than the rendering of the objects themselves.

Our visual systems, receiving under these conditions the optical inputs that they would normally receive from the corresponding three-dimensional scene, draw for us the inference for which those systems have evolved—that is, the inference that the inputs arise from that three-dimensional scene. Our visual systems do not draw the very different inference that happens to be correct in this artificially contrived situation—that is, the inference that the inputs arise from a mere simulacrum that resembles its real counterpart only when viewed from the one special vantage point.

Actually, the precise location of the viewing point (particularly if it remains monocular and stationary) is often not critical. Natural landscapes, in particular, lack the straight lines and regular shapes that sharply define the locations of vanishing points in the picture plane and, hence, the location of the optimal vantage point in the viewing space. Consequently, one can experience a remarkably good trompe-l'oeil effect in any museum or art gallery that includes large, well-illuminated, landscape paintings. Simply look at such a painting from across the room with one eye, through a sheet of paper rolled up to form a tube that restricts the view to just the painting itself. In this way, the cues (of binocular and motion parallax, surface texture, and rectangular edge) that normally inform the visual system of the flatness of the painted surface are effectively removed. In the absence of these conflicting cues, the visual system is left with essentially the information it would receive from similarly viewing the corresponding three-dimensional scene through such a tube. It is surprising how effectively what was merely a painted surface hanging on a wall then expands into the seeming reality of an unbounded, luminous three-dimensional vista.

Incidentally, some anthropologists have claimed that people raised in the uncarpentered environments of pretechnological cultures fail to recognize otherwise familiar objects and scenes when presented with two-dimensional photographs of such objects or scenes. The claim seems to require, at least, some clarification or qualification, however. If such a photograph were presented to these people under trompe-l'oeil conditions—for example, if the photograph, suitably enlarged, were viewed from a sufficient distance through one eye—then the viewer's retinal image would be identical to that arising from a similarly monocular view of the corresponding real object or scene, which, by hypothesis, is immediately recognized. Of course, the possibility remains that something that is recognized under trompe-l'oeil conditions might not be recognized when conflicting cues indicate the flat, two-dimensional nature of the visual display. Still, even monkeys reared in isolation show appropriate emotional responses to objects shown only as photographs.[20]

The lesson of the trompe l'oeil, like the lesson of depth illusions, such as *Turning the Tables* (Drawing A2), is unmistakable: Provided only that we take some care to avoid conflicting visual messages, our perceptual systems are more than ready to make the three-dimensional interpretation that the artist sought to suggest through cues that could be manipulated within the picture itself. Principally, these are cues of the following four types:

1. *Linear perspective*, in which lines that in the three-dimensional scene would be parallel to each other (but not to the picture plane) converge toward a vanishing point in the plane of the picture (as illustrated in Figure III-9b) and, correspondingly, in which objects and textural elements of a given real size are rendered appropriately smaller in accordance with what would be their greater distance behind the picture plane (as illustrated in Figure III-10a).

2. *Aerial perspective*, in which very distant objects (such as remote mountains) are painted correspondingly lighter, bluer, and with re-

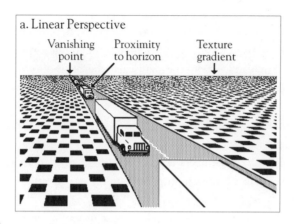

a. Linear Perspective

Vanishing point   Proximity to horizon   Texture gradient

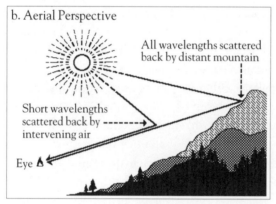

b. Aerial Perspective

All wavelengths scattered back by distant mountain

Short wavelengths scattered back by intervening air

Eye

FIGURE III-10

(a) A picture using linear perspective, in which parallel lines converge to a vanishing point (and in which the images of objects of uniform size—including textural elements—become correspondingly smaller with distance). (b) Illustration of the cause of aerial perspective, in which distant objects appear lighter and bluer because of the predominantly shorter wavelengths of sunlight scattered back to our eyes by the intervening air.

duced brightness contrast to simulate the atmospheric scattering of the shorter wavelengths of the sunlight (back to our eyes) as this sunlight passes through the intervening air (as schematized in Figure III-10b).

3. *Occultation* (also called *occlusion* by many vision scientists—though less aptly I believe), in which a closer object cuts off the view of any part of another object that is directly behind it, as is illustrated in Figure III-9a by the occultation of part of either cylinder A or cylinder C by the closer cylinder B. Accordingly, for any line of sight from the chosen viewing point, only the opaque surface that is closest to the viewing point along that line of sight is depicted in the painting; all more distant surfaces along that line of sight remain hidden.

4. *Proximity of base to horizon*, in which solid objects that are presumed to rest on the common horizontal ground (or floor) are painted with their lowest points (interpreted as their points of support by the ground) higher in the picture—that is, closer to the horizon line—if those objects are more distant from the viewer in three-dimensional space (again, see Figure III-10a).[21]

A closer, unconstrained, binocular inspection of a trompe-l'oeil painting quickly disabuses us of our initial belief that the objects we saw really exist as solid bodies in three-dimensional space. Yet, when we then back away and again view the painting from its intended vantage point, our newly gained intellectual knowledge of the two-dimensional character of the visual display may have little or no effect on the illusory appearance of three dimensionality. Our automatic machinery of visual interpretation, oblivious to the understandings of the higher intellect, may yield up, as compellingly as before, a vista of three-dimensional objects in space. The painting may still "trompe" at least the eye, if not (any longer) the "I."

In the broad context of the arts, of course, trompe-l'oeil paintings constitute an extremely limited genre. I consider them here not for their artistic or aesthetic merit but for their psychological significance. I cannot improve on Michael Kubovy's eloquent statement of how we regard what has so thoroughly deceived the visual system on which we implicitly rely in our daily lives:

> ...looking at it sends a shiver down our metaphysical spines much in the way we shiver when we think about an accident in which we were almost involved; we stare at it much as we might stare at the carcass of a wild animal that almost got the better of us. A trompe l'oeil picture is an epistemological close call...[22]

Inferential Mechanics of Perceiving

The trompe l'oeil teaches us that our visual experience is not fully determined either by what in fact is in front of us or by what we intellectually believe to be in front of us. Our visual experience evidently is the product of highly sophisticated and deeply entrenched inferential principles that operate at a level of our visual system that is quite inaccessible to conscious introspection or voluntary control. We do not first experience a two-dimensional image and then consciously calculate or infer the external three-dimensional scene that is most likely, given that image. The first thing we experience is the three-dimensional world—as our visual system has already inferred it for us on the basis of the two-dimensional input. Hermann von Helmholtz, the great nineteenth-century scientist who more than any other single individual laid the foundations for our present understanding of visual and auditory perception, expressed this by characterizing perception as "unconscious inference."[23]

Inferences, if they are to be of any use, cannot be drawn at random. They must be drawn in accordance with principles that are generally valid in the domain to which they are to be applied. An example of such a principle that is of fundamental relevance to much of what I am arguing is the principle that we do not view the world from a special vantage point. Because we are freely mobile agents, this principle is generally valid and, hence, usually leads to correct inferences from our visual inputs. Of course, when our view of the world, contrary to the premise of this principle, is constrained to a special viewing point, our perceptual systems may draw a wrong inference.

Suppose, for example, that the view we obtain through a peephole is of a small window and, behind that, a pattern of three surfaces bounded by three lines forming a fork, as schematically illustrated in Figure III-11a. According to the automatically applied principle that we are not viewing the world from a special vantage point, the three lines are inferred to belong to the same object. For, if one of the three lines belonged, say, to a more distant object, the probability that its projection would exactly intersect the junction of the other two lines of the closer object would be virtually zero. According to further principles to be mentioned later, the object to which these three lines belong (as edges) is likely to be interpreted as the corner of a cube. When, however, the window is expanded, as illustrated in Figure III-11b, we discover that

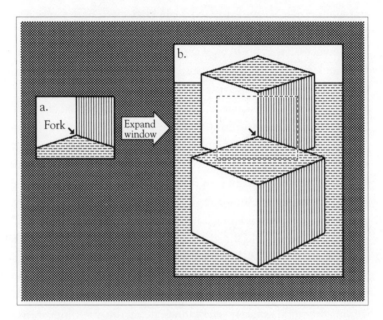

FIGURE III-11

(a) A peephole view of three lines meeting at a point behind a small window. The three lines tend to be seen as the edges of a cubical corner. (b) Expansion of the window reveals, however, that one edge belongs to a separate object situated behind the first. The apparent coincidence of the three lines depends on viewing the scene from the special vantage point enforced by the peephole.

we have been deceived. And if we are now able to change our viewing position, we discover that the vertical line, which is an edge of the more distant object, no longer intersects the junction of the lower two lines, which are edges of the closer object.

Occasionally, such coincidences can arise even under natural conditions. A certain point along a road in the foothills behind Stanford University affords the view of downtown Palo Alto shown in Figure III-12 (a black-and-white drawing that I carefully traced from the projected image of a color slide that I had taken through a telephoto lens). From this particular viewing point, Palo Alto appears to be dominated by a single tall building whose top half is oddly different from the bottom half. The illusion is destroyed by taking a few steps (for example, to the left) and thus breaking the alignment between edges at different depths. One then sees that what appeared as a single tall building is really two buildings, the Palo Alto Civic Center in front and a taller office building behind (Figure III-13).

Why our perceptual inferences have come to be so involuntary, swift, and unconscious is clear enough. In the exigencies of real life, one might otherwise run the risk of being quite literally "buried in thought." Throughout biological evolution, animals capable of more rapid and veridical (accurate and reliable) perception of the external world surely gained thereby a selective advantage in survival and reproduction. Two-dimensional retinal images have never been significant in themselves. They have been significant only as our ancestors' best available source of information for inferring what three-dimensional configurations in the external world gave rise to those retinal images.

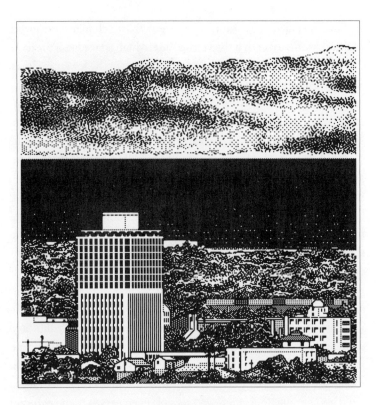

FIGURE III-12

A 1980s view of downtown Palo Alto, California, from a particular vantage point in the foothills behind Stanford University. In the lower left of this view one sees what appears to be a tall building with differently styled upper and lower halves.

The consequence is that under conditions resembling those in which the perceptual system has evolved—what we call *natural* conditions—this system operates so efficiently that we remain totally unaware of its existence, let alone of its unsurpassed sophistication and complexity. The system furnishes us with a veridical representation of what is "out there" much as if it were merely a transparent window on the world. Only through artificial conditions, such as those contrived by the perceptual psychologist, the magician, or the trompe-l'oeil artist, are we made aware of the powerful inferential work of the visual system's hidden machinery. If we could always be in direct and complete contact with what was in fact in front of us and, hence, did not have to rely on inference, we would no longer be susceptible to optical tricks and illusions. What we have called a trompe-l'oeil painting would then be experienced as exactly what it is—a pattern of colored patches on a two-dimensional surface.

Of course, perception with an absolute guarantee of veridicality was never a real possibility. Being bounded three-dimensional organisms in an unbounded three-dimensional world, we necessarily view that world, at any moment, from a localized viewing point. Moreover, even from that viewing point, we have access not to the three-dimensional structure of the world surrounding us but only to the two-dimensional image that the surrounding world projects onto our retinas at that particular viewing position. According to a fundamental theorem of topology, the relations between objects in a space of three dimensions cannot all be preserved in a two-dimensional projection. The consequence is that, as we move about, even a fixed configuration of objects

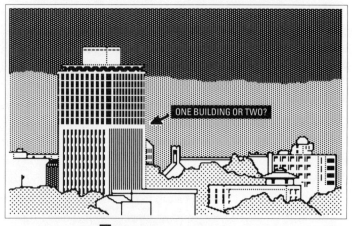

Shift vantage point

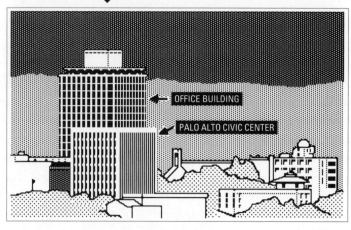

FIGURE III-13

A small (leftward) shift in the viewing position reveals that there are really two tall buildings in Figure III-12.

in space must project on the sensory surface as a changing pattern in which the subpatterns corresponding to individual objects grow larger or smaller with our shifting perspective and sometimes disappear entirely as a result of occultation by closer objects. It is ultimately the variability and incompleteness of the view afforded us by our dimensionally reduced window on the world that leave us irremediably susceptible to occasional perceptual solecisms and deceptions.

To err is human. But to err is also inherent in the existential geometry of being in the world.

Perceptual Ambiguity

What is remarkable is that we err so seldom. For, in fact, any single two-dimensional projection of the world is consistent with an infinite variety of possible three-dimensional worlds. Hence, the information from any one viewpoint is infinitely ambiguous. Figure III-14a shows how a standard cube, the concave interior of a cubical corner, and each of two differently oriented flat trompe-l'oeil renderings of the cube could all yield exactly the same retinal projection from the indicated viewing point. All that is required is that for any point in one such shape, corresponding points in each of the other shapes all fall on a single line intersecting in the viewing point. Clearly, shapes of great variety, beyond the four shown, could also be constructed to yield the same projection.

There is, moreover, no requirement that a trompe l'oeil be painted on a flat surface. In fact, any world that is alternative to the one perceived (that is alternative, in this case, to the cube) deceives the eye

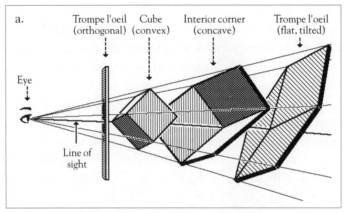

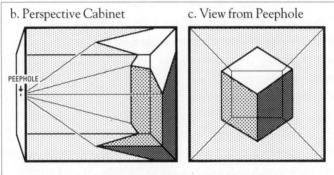

FIGURE III-14

(a) Exactly the same retinal projection can arise when, from a particular viewing position, we view quite different structures in the three-dimensional world. In the case illustrated here, the same retinal projection results from viewing a standard cube, a concave interior corner of a cube, and two flat trompe-l'oeil depictions of a cube, one at right angles (orthogonal) to our line of sight and one tipped at an arbitrary angle. (b) A perspective cabinet with walls so painted that when we look into the cabinet through a precisely positioned peephole, we receive exactly the same retinal projection we would receive if we were viewing a three-dimensional cube. (c) The illusory cube, as seen through the peephole.

and could appropriately be called a trompe-l'oeil world. In the general case, a trompe l'oeil need meet only the two essential conditions (a) that it project onto the retina a pattern of light identical to the pattern that the scene we seem to perceive would project and (b) that it nevertheless differ radically in its three-dimensional structure from that scene. It could therefore be painted on a surface of any shape, as long as each line projected from the viewing point intersects that surface (and does so first at a point that is not too close to the eye), and as long as the surface is uniformly illuminated (or, equivalently, as long as the chiaroscuro of the painting itself compensates for inhomogeneities in its illumination).

The ceiling on which Fra Andrea Pozzo painted his great trompe l'oeil in the Church of Sant'Ignazio in Rome, is in fact hemicylindrical. Pozzo carefully worked out the projection of the elaborate scene of the Ascension of Sant'Ignazio onto this curved ceiling so that a viewer who stands at the center of projection, marked by a disk of yellow marble in the floor far below, cannot tell where the real church ends and where Pozzo's loftier extension begins.

Within smaller compass, seventeenth-century artists of the Netherlands painted the interiors of boxes, called *perspective cabinets* or *peepshows*, in such a way that a monocular view of the interior of the box through the single peephole at the center of the projection yields an apparently three-dimensional vista extending far beyond the confines of the box itself. The National Gallery of London has an excellent example by Samuel van Hoogstraten. It portrays a Dutch interior with a view of a canal. The tile floor, chairs, and a dog, though painted partly on the vertical wall and partly on the horizontal floor of the perspective cabinet, appear to be continuous solid objects without bend or discontinuity at the corners of the cabinet. Indeed, to the extent that one can discern the walls and floor of the cabinet itself, they may appear as a transparent surface through which one seems to see the three-dimensional scene beyond. The principle of the perspective cabinet is schematically illustrated in Figures III-14b, which shows a cutaway view of a cabinet portraying a cube, and III-14c, which indicates how the cube would appear through the peephole.

Perhaps the ultimate tour de force of the trompe l'oeil (already suggested, to some extent, by the contemporary works of Calum Colvin and of the team of Vera Lehndorff and Holger Trülzsch) would be to take an arbitrary three-dimensional interior containing solid objects (such as tables, chairs, lamps, or even people) and to paint that interior and its objects so that when the scene is viewed from the intended vantage point, an entirely different, arbitrarily chosen scene is projected to the eye. This carries to the extreme the principle that the surface on which the trompe l'oeil is painted can be of any shape as long as it meets the stated conditions (including restriction of viewing to a peephole and appropriately uniform illumination).

The trompe l'oeil, as so far described, does not surprise us until we have inspected it closely enough or moved our viewing position far enough to discover that it is not the three-dimensional scene that it initially appeared to be. However, three-dimensional variants of the trompe l'oeil can produce astonishing anomalies from the outset. One of the best-known examples is the trapezoidal room devised by

Adalbert Ames, Jr.[24] The unconventional floor plan of such a room is shown in Figure III-15a. The room is considerably odder, however, than what can be indicated in a floor plan alone; the floor and ceiling also slope in opposite directions so that the distance from floor to ceiling may be twice as great at corner A as at corner B. All such dimensions are precisely chosen so that from the vantage point provided by the peephole, the trapezoidal room yields the same retinal projection as that yielded by a standard rectangular room. (Once again, a flat trompe-l'oeil painting or photograph, indicated by the horizontal line on the plan, could also yield that projection. Some other, quite striking three-dimensional variants of the Ames room can be viewed in the *Cité des Sciences, de l'Industrie et Technologie* in Paris.)

In the standard Ames room the perceptual anomaly is usually achieved as follows: Two people of equal stature stand in the two back corners of the trapezoidal room, in the positions marked A and B in Figure III-15a. The startling appearance of this scene viewed through the peephole is illustrated in Figure III-15b. (Photographs of such a view with two actual people can be found in many introductory psychology textbooks.) Because the person standing in corner A is much farther from the viewing point than the person standing in corner B, the image of the person at corner A that is projected on the viewer's retina (as well as on the picture plane indicated for the trompe l'oeil in the plan) may be only about half the size of that projected by the person at corner B. Moreover, the slopes of the floor and ceiling are such that persons who reach little more than halfway to the ceiling at A would find themselves jammed against the ceiling in corner B.

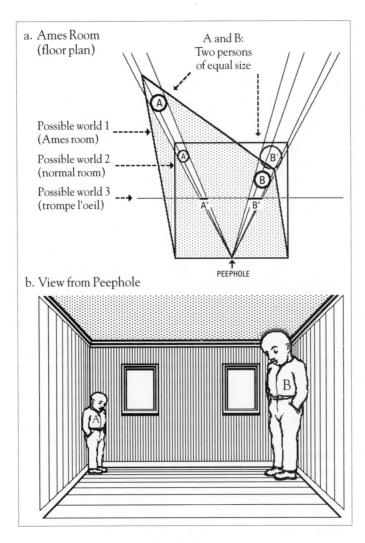

a. Ames Room
(floor plan)

A and B:
Two persons
of equal size

Possible world 1 ------→
(Ames room)

Possible world 2 ------→
(normal room)

Possible world 3 --→
(trompe l'oeil)

PEEPHOLE

b. View from Peephole

FIGURE III-15

(a) The floor plan of an Ames room, showing its unconventional trapezoidal shape and its projective equivalence to a normal, rectangular room from the special vantage point provided by the peephole. (b) The appearance, through the peephole, of the room and of two individuals, A and B, of equal size, standing in the corners.

Despite the inherent ambiguity as to which world has given rise to the input, the visual system does not for a moment entertain the alternative represented by the flat trompe l'oeil, the correct alternative represented by the trapezoidal room with sloping floor and ceiling, or any of an infinite number of other alternatives. Instead, the visual system quite automatically picks out the rectangular interpretation that would normally be the veridical one. In fact, this disambiguation, which must be based on our internalized, unconscious wisdom about the geometry of the world, is so automatic that even when the two persons standing in the two corners are well known to us, our conscious knowledge that they are in reality of equal stature has no effect on our visual experience. Whichever person stands in corner A still appears only half as tall as the one who stands in corner B.

Internalized Principles of Disambiguation

Why does the visual system select the three-dimensional interpretation in which the Ames room is (incorrectly) represented as rectangular and, hence, in which two people known to be of equal stature are represented as being of very different sizes? The answer cannot be simply that the system goes for the one interpretation that most agrees with what is already known or familiar. After all, in our previous experience, rooms have probably varied more widely in size and shape than people have.

A possible answer, which is consistent with arguments that I have for some time been making about perception,[25] is that the perceptual system has internalized the most pervasive and enduring regularities of the world. I have particularly emphasized genetic internalization through natural selection, though significant additional internalization occurs in each individual through learning. Although we cannot yet say what portion of what is internalized is internalized through evolution and what portion through learning, we must keep in mind that the principles of learning have themselves evolutionarily arisen as a genetic accommodation to regularities of the world.[26]

Whether they have been incorporated through natural selection or subsequent learning, the internalized regularities of the world may be quite abstract. If so, it is not relatively recent and specialized facts concerning the probable distributions of sizes of members of a particular, currently existing species that are most deeply internalized but rather much more general and sharply defined facts concerning, for example, the geometry of three-dimensional Euclidean space. These include the principles I have already stated—such as that light travels in straight lines and that we do not view the world from a special vantage point.

In the present context, moreover, it may be significant that rectangular corners enjoy a privileged status in the geometry of three-dimensional space. Some years ago, David Perkins and, independently, I (with a research assistant, Elizabeth Smith) undertook psychological investigations of the rules by which people infer whether or not three lines coming together at a point is the projection of a rectangular corner.[27] For mnemonic convenience, the two-dimensional projection of a junction of three lines is called a *fork* if (as in the earlier Figure III-11) none of its three angles between adjacent lines is greater than 180°, and the projection of such a junction is called an *arrow* if one of these angles does exceed 180°. The limiting cases in which two of the lines form a straight angle (that is, meet at exactly 180°) or in which two of the lines coincide with each other (that is, meet at 0°), are called a *T-junction* and an *L-junction*, respectively. Perkins and, without yet knowing of Perkins's results, Smith and I found that the ways in which people perceived these various junctions can be stated in the form of two simply stated principles, which I here refer to as *Perkins's rules* (in recognition of the fact that he had the good sense to publish first!):

1. A *fork junction* in a picture is interpreted as a rectangular corner in space if and only if each of the three angles of the fork exceeds 90°.

2. An *arrow junction* in a picture is interpreted as a rectangular corner in space if and only if each of its two smaller angles is less than 90° while the sum of those two smaller angles exceeds 90°.

(From these two rules, we can also deduce that the T-junction in a picture will be interpreted as a rectangular corner in space if and only if the third line is at right angles to the other two.)

In our experiment, Smith and I presented people with junctions formed by three lines coming together at all possible angles achievable by increments of 15°—the 61 alternative junctions arrayed in Figure III-16a. For each such junction, we asked the observers to say whether or not they perceived the junction (visible through a circular window and rotatable by the observer into any possible orientation) as the corner of a cube in three-dimensional space. The results are graphically summarized in the similarly arranged array of black circles in Figure III-16b; the size of each black circle is proportional to the numbers of individuals who indicated that they perceived the corresponding junction in Figure III-16a to be the corner of a cube.

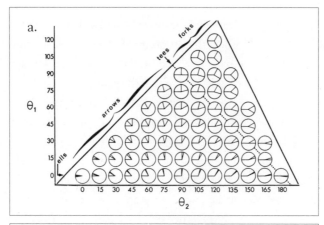

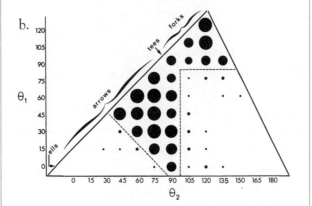

FIGURE III-16

(a) A two-dimensional array of the three-line fork and arrow junctions that subjects in the experiment by Shepard and Smith viewed (in various orientations) through a circular window. (b) The frequencies with which the subjects indicated that they saw these junctions as the corner of a cube, encoded as the size of the black circle in the corresponding location of the two-dimensional array. The broken lines demarcate the two regions of the array that could correspond to the (parallel) projection of the corner of a cube.

The two principles just stated as Perkins's rules specify two triangular subregions of this two-dimensional space—as roughly indicated by the broken lines in Figure III-16b. The upper of these two regions includes the fork junctions and the lower includes the arrow junctions that could be projections of a rectangular corner according to the geometric laws of parallel projection (that is, the laws of projection to a retinal image when the object, or cube, is very distant). That the black circles are uniformly large inside and very small outside these subregions shows that our observers were precisely tuned to what could or could not be the projection of a rectangular corner. Accordingly, I suggest that Perkins's rules are the result of an evolutionary internalization of these highly abstract and precise geometric laws of parallel projection.

For each of the 61 junctions, Smith and I also asked people whether they could perceive each such junction as a corner of each of two other (noncubical) types, namely, as the corner of a regular tetrahedron (in which each pair of lines in three-dimensional space would meet at 60°, rather than at 90°) and as the flat "corner" resembling the Mercedes-Benz symbol (in which each pair of lines would meet at the maximum possible value of 120°). The results of these further tests showed that the individuals were much less precisely tuned to such nonrectangular corners. In part, then, the reason that we experience the Ames room in the way we do may be that, having internalized the abstract laws governing the projection of the geometrically important special case of rectangular corners, we have a strong predilection to make that rectangular interpretation whenever the lines in the projection satisfy those laws. In constructing an interpretation on the basis of the two-dimensional projection available at each eye, our visual system may be seeking what a mathematician might call a *normalized* or an *orthogonalized* (that is, a right-angled) interpretation in three-dimensional space. Although many of the junctions of three lines could be the corner of a cube, the corner of a tetrahedron, the "flat" corner, or various other types of corner, people tend to perceive the corner as cubical when that is among the possibilities.

Art as Illusion

Trompe-l'oeil paintings and Ames rooms vividly make the point that our perceptual systems do not invariably show us exactly and only what is before us. Our susceptibility to illusion, ambiguity, and error is, however, not without its compensations. While uniformly veridical perception might protect us from error, it would significantly diminish the scope of the arts. Paintings could no longer transport us to ancient times, exotic places, or imaginary worlds; caricatures and cartoons could no longer whimsically capture the ridiculous aspects of persons and situations; and photographs could no longer preserve our childhoods, adventures, friends, and families through the vicissitudes of space, time, and final separation. Even film and television would be reduced to no more than a two-dimensional play of colored patterns. All forms of the graphic arts, with the arguable exception of abstract expressionism, would be lost (or reduced to a merely accidental kind of abstract expressionism). In short, we should run the risk of confronting an emptiness, expressed in Jean-Paul Sartre's *Nausea*, in which

"Things are entirely what they appear to be and *behind them*...there is nothing."[28]

Sir Ernst Gombrich long ago made an art historian's case for an inextricable connection between the two phenomena named in the title of his singularly perceptive book *Art and Illusion*.[29] I suggest that evolutionary considerations, too, indicate that art necessarily *is* illusion. In the immense history of life on earth, art is but a very recent development. Since its emergence with Homo sapiens, there has been insufficient time (and, probably, insufficient selective pressure) for the evolution of extensive neural machinery adapted specifically to the interpretation of pictures. The implication is inescapable: Pictures must appeal to us, to the extent that they do, because they engage neural machinery that had previously evolved for other purposes. These other purposes can be none other than those of making sense of biologically significant objects and events in the three-dimensional world in which our ancestors evolved. (And we must, I believe, look in the same direction for the explanation of our appreciation of other arts, including music.[30]) If this evolutionary analysis is valid, art is necessarily illusory in the following sense: It uses one thing—say, an artificial two-dimensional pattern—to excite neural circuits that have evolved to represent something else—namely, natural objects and events in a three-dimensional world.

Perceptual ambiguity can of course be, at least, inconvenient—as when we cannot tell whether the dark shape looming ahead of us along a trail at night is a bush or a bear, or whether the announcement in a hastily written note is "Have gone for food" or "Have gone for good."

Yet, ambiguity is the principal source of the inexhaustible richness of art. If we do not quickly tire of a picture or a piece of music, it is because we do not always see exactly the same pattern of colored patches or hear the same pattern of tonal pitches. Instead, we pick up or resonate each time to somewhat different relations within the pattern. Of course, our enjoyment may also persist because the picture or the music recreates, within us, a setting and mood that we enjoyed on another occasion. But this, too, is a manifestation of ambiguity. The picture or music, however aesthetically pleasing in its own right, is not only interpretable as an abstract pattern of patches in space or pitches in time; the picture or music is also interpretable as, say, the play of moonlight and of violins over lapping waters on the shore of some distant summer's eve.

Pictorial versus Ecological Perception

In talking of unconscious inference and of our susceptibility to illusion, ambiguity, and error, I have so far slighted a remarkable fact, emphasized by the late perceptual psychologist James J. Gibson:[31] Under normal conditions of unobstructed, binocular viewing and good illumination, our visual perception is virtually 100% veridical. According to Gibson, the perceptual significance of illusions and ambiguities have been greatly exaggerated. Such phenomena, though they may help to enliven a lecture in introductory psychology, are rare, Gibson held, except under highly artificial conditions—such as those that are set up in the darkened laboratory or lecture hall or those that (as in the case of the magician's cabinet, the perspective cabinet, or the Ames room) more or less dictate one's viewing position. Under contrasting natural, or in Gibson's terminology—*ecologically valid*, conditions—the information available at an individual's freely mobile viewing position is sufficient to specify the surrounding layout and to permit what Gibson called *direct perception* of that layout. Although the information available from any one viewpoint may be compatible with an infinite variety of possible worlds, the information afforded by the different viewpoints traversed by the moving observer is compatible with only one.

Gibson's point is of indisputable validity and importance in relation to perception under viewing conditions that are both natural and favorable. The fact that we usually manage as well as we do in the three-dimensional world surely attests to the adequacy of the information that is available under such conditions. However, the fact of this adequacy does not in itself provide answers to all questions that cognitive, behavioral, and neural scientists consider significant: In what form is the relevant information contained in the pattern of light available from a mobile observer's viewpoint? By what neural processes does the visual system extract this information from this pattern? And, most pertinently here, what does happen under poorly illuminated, partially obstructed, interrupted, or in some way constrained or unnatural conditions of viewing? Gibson and his followers have made a promising beginning toward providing answers to the first of these three questions. But their characterization of perception as "direct," and their consequent rejection of the notion that the visual system constructs an internal representation of the external world has discouraged their pursuit of the second question and has hobbled their approach to the third.

Even nature sometimes affords only brief, partial, or inadequately lighted glimpses of objects and events of life-and-death significance. And, as illustrated in Figure III-12, improbable alignments can sometimes arise by chance. Moreover, with the evolutionarily recent advent of human arts and technologies, conditions that depart quite radically from the conditions prevailing for our remote ancestors can no longer be considered rare. Of particular relevance are the conditions—highly unnatural in this evolutionary sense—that we call looking at pictures. Whether or not we consider the viewing of pictures to be an ecologically valid activity, it is certainly an activity that is enjoyed by many people and that for a few (including artists and critics and historians of art) may even become life's dominant preoccupation.

Gibson's account of how we are able to perceive a three-dimensional layout veridically when we are free to move about does not explain why, when our view *is* artificially constrained to a fixed viewpoint, we experience only one of the infinite number of possible worlds compatible with the projection at that viewpoint. In my discussion of the Ames room, I suggested that the selection of the rectangularly shaped alternative, out of all possible interpretations, was based on some internalized unconscious wisdom about very general and quite abstract, geometric properties of the world. I now further suggest that while Ames rooms may indeed be highly contrived and rarely encountered objects in our environment, the internalized principles underlying our perceptual interpretation of an Ames room (if we ever encounter one) are the same principles that underlie our perceptual interpretation of pictures (which we encounter virtually every day).

Unlike a person peering into a perspective cabinet or an Ames room, of course, a person viewing a picture is, as a person viewing a natural three-dimensional scene, free to move to different viewing positions. For the viewer of a picture, however, the transformations in the available projection that are induced by such shifts in viewing position will not be the same as the transformations that would result if the picture had been replaced by the corresponding three-dimensional scene. This is, in part, why we are not deceived; why we perceive the picture, unlike a trompe-l'oeil painting, as a two-dimensional picture and not, literally, as a three-dimensional vista.

As I have noted, a picture portraying a three-dimensional scene implicitly provides its own peephole. Yet, the retinal image produced by a picture will be identical to the retinal image that would arise from the corresponding three-dimensional scene only when the picture itself is viewed from the unique vantage point adopted by the artist. Remarkably, in viewing ordinary pictures, we experience relatively little distortion even when we view a picture from a position displaced appreciably from the viewing position of the artist (or of the camera, as when we watch a movie from one side of the theater). The explanation of this remarkable fact, first developed by Maurice Henri Pirenne (apparently partly on the basis of a suggestion received from Albert Einstein at the end of his life), appears to be roughly as follows:[32]

First, on the basis of the information ordinarily available from the texture and edges of the flat surface on which the picture is painted, printed, or projected, the visual system computes the relative distance and slant of that two-dimensional surface (just as it does for any surface in the visual field). Next, the system uses this computed information about the spatial disposition of the surface to compensate for the distortion in the retinal projection of the slanting picture that is caused by any deviation of the viewer from the vantage point implied by the perspective in the picture itself. Finally, having thus compensated for the slant of the picture, the visual system constructs a correct representation of the portrayed three-dimensional scene, just as if it had viewed the picture, unslanted, from its correct vantage point.

What happens under the very different conditions of the trompe l'oeil provides further evidence for this surprisingly sophisticated, multistage process of visual interpretation: A trompe-l'oeil painting that appears vividly three-dimensional and real when viewed from the correct vantage point may appear grossly distorted and unreal when viewed from a very different position. Thus the upward architectural extension of the Church of Sant'Ignazio depicted in Pozzo's ceiling appears to tip away from vertical, almost as if the building were collapsing, when viewed far from the yellow disk in the floor that marks the correct viewing position.[33] According to Pirenne's theory, such apparent distortion arises because the visual system, lacking access (under these trompe-l'oeil conditions) to information about the disposition of the two-dimensional surface itself, is unable to correct for a displacement from the correct viewing position and hence is unable to construct a representation of the portrayed three-dimensional scene that is invariant under shifts of viewpoint. Under ordinary circumstances of picture viewing, then, the visual information about the surface on which a picture is painted, printed, or projected has two opposing effects: It decreases the deceptive three-dimensional reality of the portrayed scene from what is achievable under trompe-l'oeil conditions when the picture is viewed from the correct vantage point; but at the same time, it increases the robustness or invariance of the three-dimensional interpretation of the picture under deviations from the perspectively correct vantage point.

Pirenne provided a striking illustration of the relevant principles in a single photograph (Figure III-17).[34] It is, in fact, a photographic example of pictorial self-reference. In it, we see smiling United States presidential aspirant Richard Nixon and, behind and above him—but at a considerable slant with respect to the camera's viewpoint—an enlarged, earlier photograph of a similarly smiling Nixon. But the photograph of Nixon himself, which I shall refer to as his *first-order* photograph, and the earlier photograph of Nixon contained in that first-order photograph, which I shall refer to as his *second-order* photograph, are remarkably different in visual appearance.

In the first-order photograph, Nixon appears in his normal, three-dimensional shape. Moreover, this normal appearance remains regardless of the angle from which we view the first-order photograph (that is, the slant at which we hold the opened page of this book). In the second-order photograph, however, Nixon appears flat and markedly distorted. Moreover, this same distorted appearance remains regardless of the angle from which we view the page—including the particular angle that exactly corrects for the slant of the second-order image. So even when the retinal image is exactly like the one that would be produced by the actual, three-dimensional Nixon, we see a flat and oddly distorted image of Nixon. Apparently, as both Pirenne and Kubovy have

FIGURE III-17

A photographic example of pictorial self-reference, showing United States presidential aspirant Richard Nixon and, also, an earlier, enlarged photograph of Nixon. Pirenne pointed out that the first-order image of Nixon appears normal whereas the second-order image of Nixon (the photograph of the photograph) appears distorted and, further, that this remains true regardless of the angle from which we view the entire picture. (From World Wide Photos, Inc.)

concluded from such examples, our visual system is able to correct for only one slant at a time. The frame and texture formed by the physical page on which the first-order photograph is printed dominates and, hence, determines the correction for slant. A second-order photograph within that first-order photograph is therefore left distorted and flat in appearance, regardless of the viewing angle.

How did the human visual system acquire this impressive ability to compensate for the slant of a picture and, thus, to form the same, correct impression of the three-dimensional scene portrayed almost regardless of viewing position? One might be tempted to doubt my earlier supposition that humankind has not been making pictures long enough for the evolution of mechanisms specifically tailored to the interpretation of pictures. However, there are reasons to suppose that the corrective mechanism advanced by Pirenne would have been useful to our remote ancestors long before those ancestors took to making pictures. Such a mechanism would greatly facilitate the identification of significant objects (including prey, predators, and conspecifics) from their characteristic surface markings, regardless of the orientations in which such objects were seen.

The uses to which humans have come to make of such a mechanism are, however, quite far removed from the uses for which the mechanism originally evolved. Kubovy puts forward the intriguing conjecture that such Renaissance painters as Andrea Mantegna and Leonardo da Vinci intentionally designed the perspective of certain religious frescoes so that the correct vantage point is well above the head of any viewer standing on the floor of the church. The purpose of this deliberate de-

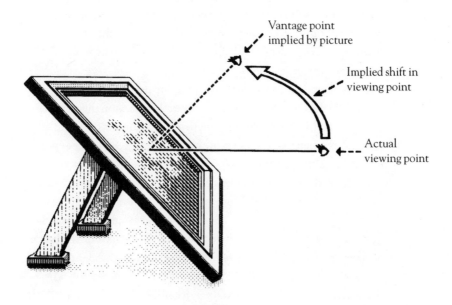

Vantage point
implied by picture

Implied shift in
viewing point

Actual
viewing point

FIGURE III-18

Two positions from which a picture might be viewed. Only one such viewing position can correspond to the vantage point of the artist and, hence, yield a retinal image identical to the image that would result from viewing the three-dimensional scene portrayed in the picture.

parture from what would seem to be a correct application of the rules of perspective, Kubovy suggests, was to induce a feeling of spirituality in the viewers. As a result of their visual systems' automatic computation of the above-their-heads location of the implied vantage point, such viewers may gain an unarticulated awareness that, tied as they still are to their earth-bound mortal bodies, they remain below the implied, loftier level of immortal spirituality and grace. Or even, as Kubovy suggests, as a result of a subjective elevation of their egocenters to that implied loftier vantage point, they may already experience some foretaste of the long-promised freeing of soul from body.[35]

In any event, the two-dimensional perspective representation of a three-dimensional scene necessarily implies a particular vantage point in the three-dimensional viewing space of the picture. In the case of ordinary pictures, viewers are not of course physically constrained to assume this vantage point, in the way that they may be in the case of Ames rooms, perspective cabinets, or some trompe-l'oeil paintings. Their perceptual response is nevertheless based on an unconscious computation, by their visual system, of the location of this implied vantage point. The result is that almost regardless of the angle from which they view the picture, they experience the scene as if they were viewing it from the artist's unique vantage point. (See Figure III-18.) In considering the perception of pictures, then, we cannot get away from the notion of a fixed vantage point. In fact, as I have explained in discussing my own drawings, most of the ways in which these drawings achieve ambiguity or anomaly depend, crucially, on the existence of this implied vantage point.

Resonance to Significant Objects

The human activities of creating and of looking at pictures raise questions that differ somewhat from the questions usually asked by those investigating perception under natural, ecologically valid conditions. Why do we engage in these artificial activities? Why, that is, do pictures appeal to us? And what determines why some pictures appeal to us more than others? At this point the scientists' world of the objective must, it seems, make room for the subjective. We must establish what the Gestalt psychologist Wolfgang Köhler called, in the title of his book, "The Place of Value in a World of Facts."[36] For, while perceptual psychologists may still disagree about the extent to which our experience of the world is determined by the physical input and by our internalized interpretive principles, they must surely agree that beauty, at least, is "in the eye of the beholder."

I have already indicated the general direction in which I would seek to answer such questions of aesthetics: We create pictures or look at them to the extent that they excite neural circuits that would be excited by objects or events that have been especially significant to our ancestors over evolutionary history. However, we still need to consider what classes of objects and events might have been of such great and uniform significance that neural circuits that resonate specifically to them would have attained a dominating role in the mental machinery that our ancestors have passed on to us.

Particular objects and events that were significant for the survival and reproduction of our ancestors are obvious enough. Some of these posed a potential threat: predatory and venomous animals as well as enraged or warring conspecifics; sheer precipices and yawning chasms; rampant fires, towering waves, and torrential cataracts; and the manifestations of disease, infection, death, and decay. These do not necessarily make for pretty pictures. But pictures do not have to be pretty to grab our attention; some images fascinate us just because they represent things that are threatening. We are alive today precisely because our ancestors were properly attentive to such threats. Indeed, there is reason to believe that the perceptual circuits that we have inherited from these ancestors are innately tuned to some of these things and, also, have an innate connection with appropriate emotional responses. For example, very young human infants react to a looming visual stimulus,[37] and juvenile monkeys raised in captivity exhibit a fear response when a snake is introduced into their cage for the first time.[38] More to the point, the fear elicited by the visual presence of the snake, while causing the monkeys to put a safe distance between themselves and the intruder, also motivates them to continue to maintain a close and evidently fascinated observation of it.

Equally understandable is our tendency to look at portrayals of objects that have provided more salutary indications of our security and reproductive success: a mother's loving face, a nubile body. Again, observations of primates have shown that when they are given the opportunity to look at different things, they will spend most time looking at other members of their own species. Not surprisingly, in view of the value of facial gestures for predicting the ensuing behavior of conspecifics toward oneself, recordings of eye fixations have revealed that primates tend to spend most time looking at the face and, particularly, the

FIGURE III-19

Interpretations of natural and artificial objects as facelike, including, in the lower right, my reconstruction of the hallucinatory distortion of a door latch as a face, which I experienced once when I was running a high fever.

eyes. Further, neurophysiological investigations have established that a large number of cells in the visual areas of the cortex fire only in the presence of something that is a face or, at least, sufficiently facelike. (As I have mentioned, most such cells respond maximally to a full-face view, somewhat fewer respond to a profile view, and still fewer to other views.) [39] Finally, of course, a facelike object will elicit an orienting response and smiling in a human infant —but only if the object is sufficiently like a face in the arrangement of its features.[40] It is little wonder, then, that artists have so consistently been preoccupied with the human body and, especially, the human face.

Still another indication that our heads are filled with circuits tuned to the human face is our tendency to "see" faces in the most diverse objects around us—in a house, a vehicle, or a cloud (see *a*, *b*, and *c* in Figure III-19), or even simply in the dark, as in the hypnagogic imagery experienced (particularly by young children) while falling asleep and, of course, as in our dreams. Altered states of the brain induced by sleep deprivation, psychotropic drugs, or fever evidently heighten the irritability of such circuits and thereby increase the likelihood that these circuits will become active in the absence of a corresponding external object or, at least, in the presence of an external object that only slightly resembles a face. Once while running a high fever, I experienced the door knobs and latch tongue of my partly open bedroom door as composing a funny face that alternately grimaced and protruded its tongue at me (Figure III-19d).

How, though, are we to explain the interest that many of us have in creating or in looking at pictures that are not very representational, that are to various degrees abstracted or transformed away from familiar objects and scenes? Presumably, a degree of curiosity and an inclination to explore novel stimuli was also advantageous to our ancestors, in better preparing themselves for possibly significant future turns of events. As implied in my comments on the anomalies that I called transmogrifications, an object that is novel and yet similar to an already significant object may especially warrant our close attention. We need to know how far something can depart from its usual or expected form and still have the consequences that we have found to follow from its "natural kind."[41] In doing so, we also come closer to an understanding of the critical features of a stimulus that elicits a resonant response within us and, thus, closer to an understanding of ourselves. As I also suggested in my discussion of transmogrifications, the constructions, deconstructions, and reconstructions of the the human form and human face by Picasso and other modern artists might be interpreted in this way.

Resonance to Spatial Symmetries

But what about the appeal that completely abstract designs have for us and for primitive artisans in cultures around the world? The repeating, purely geometric patterns that decorate baskets, pottery, rugs, wood carvings, floor tiles, wallpaper, public buildings, and the works of many modern artists (including, of course, practitioners of op art) do not appear to bear any resemblance to faces, bodies, animals, or natural scenes. From what evolutionary source do such abstract patterns derive their appeal?

I suggest that this appeal, too, reflects the internalization of certain pervasive properties of the world in which we have evolved. Such properties, though much more abstract than particular physical objects, are likely to have been at least as important for our survival. One such abstract property is the high probability that symmetrical or spatially repeating elements of a visual input belong to the same external object. Bilateral symmetry is a common feature of most living things (people and other mammals, birds, fish, insects, leaves, and so on) as well as of many human artifacts (boats, chairs, forks, articles of clothing, and so on). Moreover, any of the numerous objects approximating rotational symmetry (such as an apple, a pear, a pancake, a bowl, or a pencil) yields a bilaterally symmetric retinal image regardless of the angle from which the object is viewed. In contrast, the retinal images of the spaces between objects will be symmetrical only under highly improbable conditions of viewing. Accordingly, symmetries in a visual input provide powerful guides to its proper segregation into figure and ground. Some of my figure-ground ambiguities—especially, *Les Objets d'Art Surréels*, *Beckoning Balusters*, and *Wrangling Rungs* (Drawings D3, D4, and D9)—illustrate how bilateral symmetry of the boundary of a region can bias us toward the perceptual interpretation of that region as figure.

The prevalence of symmetries in significant objects is not, however, the only reason for us to have become highly responsive to symmetries in our visual inputs. A still more abstract and pervasive property of the world that, accordingly, may have become still more deeply entrenched in our visual systems is the geometry of three-dimensional Euclidean space and the associated kinematic geometry that constrains the ways in which extended objects can move in that space. Our ancestors survived and reproduced not only because they could segregate figure from ground or because they preferred to avoid some thus segregated objects and and to approach others. They were successful in avoiding, in approaching, or in manipulating such objects because they had internalized the spatial and kinematic geometry of the three-dimensional world. Surely, a hunter-gatherer who could not find the way back to the family or tribe, who could not arrange limbs and boughs to form a shelter, who could not retrieve hidden food when hungry or an infant when a predator approached would not be likely to pass on his or her genes to many descendants. Results of experiments on mental rotation and visual apparent motion have led me to conclude that our visual systems have internalized the highly abstract principles of kinematic geometry.[42]

Would the internalization of such principles explain the appeal of purely static patterns that are in some way regular, repeating, or symmetrical? The first point to note is that the defining property of such patterns is precisely that they are self-congruent under certain rigid motions. Thus, a circle and a sphere are the most symmetrical of shapes (in two and three dimensions, respectively) because each remains congruent with itself under all rigid rotations about its center. A square and a cube, though not congruent with themselves under all rotations, become congruent under certain rotations (for example, through multiples of 90° about certain axes). Similarly, infinitely repeating two-dimensional patterns, such as a checkerboard, honeycomb, or triangular tessellation, are defined by the property that they are brought into congruence with themselves not only by rotations through multiples of certain angles (90°, 60°, and 120°) but also under translations through multiples of certain distances (determined by the size of the square, hexagon, or triangle, respectively). Elsewhere, I have conjectured that our perception of shape itself may be based on the implicit computation of the self-similarity of an object under all possible rigid transformations of the object.[43] If this conjecture is true, a symmetrical or infinitely repeating pattern tends to produce extensive excitation in those neural circuits that register the self-congruence that would result from such motions. Massive neuronal resonance to symmetry, then, may be a consequence of our deep internalization of the abstract principles of kinematic geometry and may explain the ubiquitous emergence of symmetrical and repeating patterns in the artistic productions of all human cultures.

Such resonant circuits might sometimes "ring" spontaneously as a result of heightened excitability or in partial resonance to an undifferentiated stimulus—much as an undamped string of a piano may briefly sing its own characteristic note in response to a loud but nonmusical external noise. Under suitable conditions, then, we might manifest a tendency toward the spontaneous experience of abstract, geometrically regular visual patterns, just as toward the spontaneous experience of certain significant objects, such as faces. In fact, we do. In hypnagogic and hypnopompic states, as a result of sleep deprivation, drugs, or fever and, indeed, when merely stimulated by a homogeneous field of light flickering at about the frequency of alpha waves in the brain (8 to 12 Hz, or cycles per second), visual patterns emerge that are self-congruent under translation (for example, checkerboard, honeycomb, and plaid patterns), under rotation (for example, mandala, concentric, and spider-web patterns), and under a combination of rotation and translation in depth (for example, helical, spiral, and vortical or tunnel patterns). Indeed, these are just the *form constants* that Heinrich Klüver, identified in his studies of the hallucinatory effects of the drug mescaline.[44]

As noted in the autobiographical portion of the Foreword, my own experiences of spontaneous, geometrically regular patterns have primarily occurred, just as a number of my scientific and artistic ideas, in the hypnopompic state of transition from sleep to waking. Along with the one illustrated in the Foreword (Figure I-10), six of these are roughly indicated in Figure III-20. (Only two of the six original images—those shown in Figure III-20c—were experienced purely in black and white. More accurate, full-color reproductions of the original reconstructions are published elsewhere.[45]) Represented among these six images are all three of the regular tessellations of the plane: the square or rhombic, the triangular, and the hexagonal.

Subsequent tests of my ability to reconstruct from memory two similar colored repeating patterns that a graphic artist had prepared for this purpose but that I had not seen until my wife presented each to me (on two separate mornings) for four seconds each, just upon awakening, suggested that my reconstructions of the spontaneously experienced hypnopompic images approximated in Figure III-20 may be quite accurate.[46] (Admittedly, the test is not conclusive. For one thing, I was not in a hypnopompic state during the presentation of the test patterns.)

FIGURE III-20a

Black-and-white renderings of the six geometrically regular hypnopompic images that I experienced and reconstructed between 1970 and 1977.

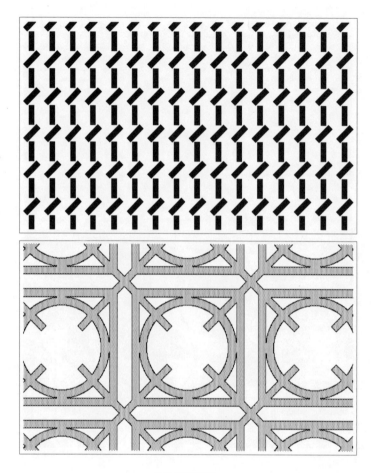

FIGURE III-20b

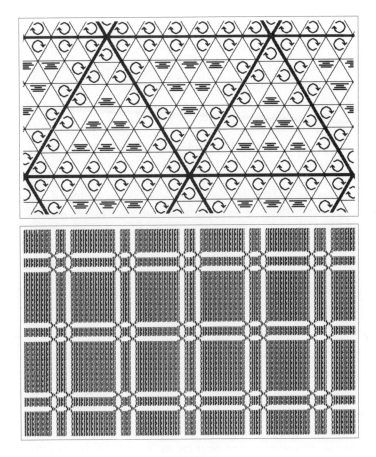

FIGURE III-20c

John Herschel, who (as I noted) reported experiencing similarly geometrically regular spontaneous images over 100 years ago, raised an interesting question about the "kaleidoscopic power" of the brain that spontaneously experienced geometrically regular images seem to reveal. I cannot do better than to quote Herschel himself:

> Now the question at once presents itself—what are these Geometrical Spectres? and how, and in what department of the bodily or mental economy do they originate?… If it be true that the conception of a regular geometrical pattern implies the exercise of thought and intelligence, it would almost seem that in such cases…we have evidence of a *thought*, an intelligence, working within our own organisation distinct from that of our own personality… in a matter so entirely abstract, so completely devoid of any moral or emotional bearing, as the production of a geometrical figure, we, as it were, seize upon (a creative and directive) principle in the very act, and in the performance of its office.[47]

That a number of scientific insights have been achieved through the visualization of a regular, repeating, or symmetrical pattern in space may not be accidental. Notable examples include Friedrich Kekulé's discovery of the hexagonal structure of the benzene molecule through a spontaneous image that he likened to a snake swallowing its own tail (of which my Drawing G7 is a variant); Nikola Tesla's invention of the induction motor following a spontaneous image of the circular rotation of a symmetrical magnetic field; and James Clerk Maxwell's formulation of the laws of electromagnetism after concretely visualizing the magnetic field as a pattern of counterrotating cylinders and balls, filling all space (in a regular, hexagonal tessellation somewhat resembling that depicted here in Figure III-20b).[48]

Such latent kaleidoscopic powers of the brain are perhaps most likely to manifest themselves when we are neither completely unconscious nor fully engaged in the ongoing analysis of sensory inputs. These powers may tend to emerge, that is, when we are in transitional hypnagogic or hypnopompic states between sleep and wakefulness or, while asleep, when we are dreaming or, while awake, when we are daydreaming. This may help to explain the observation that scientific insights have often been reported to have occurred in such states.[49]

Beyond the symmetries associated with rigid translations and rotations in space, there is also the more abstract symmetry of scale invariance that characterizes the fractal patterns of Benoit Mandelbrot.[50] Such patterns, which present essentially the same appearance at any degree of magnification, are characteristic of such natural features of the world as the shapes of coastlines, mountain ranges, forests and trees. For this reason, fractal geometry is currently making a significant contribution to the realism of computer-generated images of natural scenes. Possibly, the visual appeal of scale-invariant patterns may stem from their connections both with natural features of the physical world in which we have evolved and (as I suggested in discussing the spatial repetitions and symmetries in my own drawings) with the spatial transformations (including dilations and contractions) dictated by the kinematic geometry of the three-dimensional space in which we have evolved.

CONCLUDING REMARKS

The illusions, ambiguities, and other visual anomalies that have been explored by artists and by perceptual psychologists are not manifestations of arbitrary quirks, glitches, or design faults of the human visual system. Rather, these perceptual aberrations arise from the operation of powerful and automatic inferential principles that are well tuned to the general properties of the natural world. We owe our very existence to the effectiveness with which these principles have served all our ancestors.

One has to contrive rather special visual displays in order to bring about illusions, ambiguities, and other visual anomalies. There are two compelling reasons to investigate how the visual/cognitive system responds to such contrived conditions. First, such conditions can serve as particularly informative probes of the properties of the system that in more natural conditions operates so effectively that its own inner constraints or internalized structures remain invisible. Second, because the interpretation of two-dimensional pictures is not an activity for which we have been specifically prepared by our eons of evolution in a nonpictorial, three-dimensional world, we cannot hope for an adequate psychology of art without a close consideration of the ecologically deviant activity of looking at pictures. Taken together, these two reasons motivate the consideration of anomalous pictures as probes of the visual/cognitive system.

If perception were always direct and veridical, we would not be subject to illusions, ambiguities, and anomalies. To extend the aphorism of

Bishop Butler, we might then say not only that "everything is what it is, and not another thing,"[51] but also that everything is what it *appears to be*, and not another thing. Because we are inherently restricted to a two-dimensional projection of the three-dimensional world, however, our representation of that world must be internally constructed on the basis of the information available in that projection. True, this construction generally becomes veridical when, under the unobstructed and well-illuminated natural conditions that Gibson called ecologically valid, we are each free to move about, thereby gaining different perspectives on the world.

We have seen, however, that independent of the position from which we choose to view it, a picture carries with it its own implicit vantage point. As a consequence, such a picture does not allow us the same kind of free mobility with respect to the portrayed scene that we would enjoy in the presence of the corresponding three-dimensional scene itself. But this same limitation of a picture provides us with a convenient way of achieving informative deviations from ecologically valid conditions, without having actually to construct a three-dimensional display chamber, perspective cabinet, or Ames room, to which each viewer would then have to travel (physically) to peer, one at a time, through its fixed peephole.

In short, while a picture affords what is in some ways a rather limited window on the world, it affords what can be an informative window on the mind. We may look into that window as through a glass darkly, but what we are beginning to discern there looks very much like a reflection of the world.

N O T E S

1.   Michael Kubovy has made essentially this point in his insightful book *The Psychology of Perspective and Renaissance Art* (Cambridge: Cambridge University Press, 1986), 77.

2.   R. N. Shepard, "A possible evolutionary basis for trichromacy" (Paper presented at the SPSE/SPIE Symposium on Electronic Imaging, Santa Clara, CA, Feb. 11-16, 1990).

3.   P. Vitruvius (ca. 30 B.C.), *De archetectura*, trans. F. Granger (New York: Putnam, 1931).

4.   M. H. Pirenne, *Optics, Painting, & Photography* (Cambridge: Cambridge University Press, 1970), 152 ff.

5.   My drawings presented herein as E1, G2, and G5 (in Part II) appear on pages 90-91 of the catalogue of the exhibition: I. Sakane, ed., *A Museum of Fun: Part II* (Tokyo: The Asahi Shimbun, 1984).

6.   My drawing here designated G2 appeared on page 3 of the May 1984 issue of *Ylem: Artists Using Science and Technology* (Vol. 4, No. 1). Drawings D9 and E1 appeared on page 9 of an article, "Patterns when we wake, objects spinning in space: Shepard studies symmetry," in the July 25, 1984, issue of the Stanford University *Campus Report*. Drawings C1, D4, E3, E5, F1, G1, G4, H4, and I2 then appeared (along with Drawing E1) in R. N. Shepard "T'is a puzzlement." *The Stanford Magazine*, (1984): *12* (No. 4), 36-37. (Drawings C1, D4, and E1 subsequently appeared, also, on page 104 in J. McDermott "Researchers find there is more to vision than meets the eye," *Smithsonian*, 16 [1985]: 96-107.)

7.   My daughter Shenna had T-shirts imprinted with my anomalous elephant (Drawing E1) while she was a student at Tufts University, whose mascot was the elephant Jumbo. The word *TUFTS* was printed under the anomalous elephant in letters that were also anomalous (depth impossibility), which I had formed for this purpose.

8.   R. N. Shepard and J. Metzler, "Mental rotation of three-dimensional objects," *Science* 171 (1971): 701-703. For a nontechnical overview of this and subsequent work on mental rotation, see L. A. Cooper and R. N. Shepard, "Turning something over in the mind," *Scientific American* 251 (1984): 106-114; for more extensive coverage, see R. N. Shepard and L. A. Cooper, *Mental Images and Their Transformations* (Cambridge, MA: MIT Press/Bradford Books, 1982).

9.   S. Shepard and D. Metzler, "Mental rotation: Effects of dimensionality and type of task," *Journal of Experimental Psychology: Human Perception and Performance* 14 (1988): 3-11.

10. E. H. Carlton and R. N. Shepard, "Psychologically simple motions as geodesic paths: I. Asymmetric objects. II. Symmetric objects," *Journal of Mathematical Psychology*, in press. For earlier and less technical statements of the idea, see R. N. Shepard, "Psychophysical complementarity," in *Perceptual Organization*, ed. M. Kubovy and J. Pomerantz (Hillsdale, NJ: Lawrence Erlbaum Associates, 1981): 279-341; and R. N. Shepard, "Ecological constraints on internal representation: Resonant kinematics of perceiving, imagining, thinking, and dreaming," *Psychological Review* 91 (1984): 417-447.

11. R. N. Shepard, "Circularity in judgments of relative pitch," *Journal of the Acoustical Society of America* 36 (1964): 2346-2353. R. N. Shepard and E. Zajac, *A Pair of Paradoxes* (Murray Hill, NJ: Bell Telephone Laboratories, 1965). The latter is a computer-generated, 16-mm sound film—to our knowledge, the first film to be produced in which both the animation and the sound were generated by computer.

12. J. Freyd, "Dynamic mental representations," *Psychological Review* 94 (1987): 427-438.

13. R. N. Shepard, "Externalization of mental images and the act of creation," in *Visual Learning, Thinking, and Communication*, ed. B. S. Randhawa and W. E. Coffman (New York: Academic Press, 1978), 133-189. See pages 171ff. and, especially, the color plates between pages 176 and 177.

14. Sir J. F. W. Herschel, *Familiar Lectures on Scientific Subjects* (London: Strahan, 1867). See Herschel's lecture, "On sensorial vision."

15. See R. N. Shepard and L. A. Cooper, *Mental Images and their Transformations*, 19-23, for a historical note on the origin of the mental rotation paradigm.

16. These are the computer-generated perspective views of three-dimensional objects used for my first experiment, with Jacqueline Metzler, on mental rotation. See Note 8 above.

17. J. Jastrow, *Fact and Fable in Psychology* (New York: Houghton-Mifflin, 1900), 295. Also see his earlier article: J. Jastrow, "The mind's eye," *Popular Science Monthly* 54 (1899): 299-312.

18. L. Wittgenstein, *Philosophical Investigations*, trans. G. E. M. Anscombe (New York: Macmillan, 1953), 194.

1. See page 298 of R. N. Shepard, "Psychophysical complementarity," in *Perceptual organization*, ed. M. Kubovy and J. Pomerantz (Hillsdale, NJ: Lawrence Erlbaum Associates, 1981), 279-341. (The places where other drawings in Part II first appeared are listed in Note 6 for Part I.)

2. E. Hering, *Beitrage zur Psychologie*, Vol. 1 (Leipzig: Engleman, 1861).

3. R. M. Pirsig, *Zen and the Art of Motorcycle Maintenance* (New York: William Morrow and Company, 1974).

4. S. Kim, *Inversions* (Peterborough, NH: BYTE Books, 1981). Reprinted by W. H. Freeman, 1989.

5. Subsequently, Scott Kim devised a related but globally more successful figure-ground effect in which both the black and complementary white portions spell *figure*—as is appropriate, because whichever portion is seen is experienced as the figure. See S. Kim, *Inversions*, 36.

6. M. Kubovy and J. Psotka, "Of even, odd, and even odder numbers: The psychology of seven and spontaneity" (Paper presented at the Forty-fifth Annual Meeting of the Eastern Psychological Association, Philadelphia, Apr. 18-20, 1974).

7. L. S. Penrose and R. Penrose, "Impossible objects: A special type of visual illusion," *British Journal of Psychology* 49 (1958): 31-33 (Figure 3 on page 32). My Drawing F3 (inspired by their Figure 3) first appeared on page 646 of R. N. Shepard, "Demonstrations of circular components of pitch," *Journal of the Audio Engineering Society* 31 (1983): 641-649.

8. I. Peterson, *The Mathematical Tourist* (New York: W. H. Freeman, 1988), 120-121.

9. My poem, *Plaint*, appeared (albeit with two misprints) in the Autumn 1982 issue of the Stanford literary magazine *Sequoia* (page 62). (I don't know whether it counts as any sort of "poetic justice," but Howard Moss, then poetry editor of the *New Yorker*—which had previously declined to publish my poem, found his own interview with *Sequoia*, and his photograph, permanently bound together with my poem in the same issue of that literary magazine.)

NOTES FOR PART III

1. J. J. Gibson, *The Senses Considered as Perceptual Systems* (Boston, MA: Houghton-Mifflin, 1966); J. J. Gibson, *The Ecological Approach to Visual Perception* (Boston: Houghton-Mifflin, 1979).

2. D. Klopfer and L. A. Cooper, "Using apparent motion to measure the structure of perceived space" (Paper presented at the Twenty-sixth Annual Meeting of the Psychonomic Society, Boston, MA, Nov. 22, 1985).

3. I am using the astronomers' term *occultation* in preference to the visual scientists' term *occlusion*, which seems to me less appropriate.

4. R. L. Gregory, "Visual illusions," in *New Horizons in Psychology*, ed. B. M. Foss (Harmondsworth, U.K.: Penguin Books, 1966); R. L. Gregory, *The Intelligent Eye* (New York: McGraw-Hill, 1970).

5. See, for example, L. Kaufman, *Perception: The World Transformed* (New York: Oxford University Press, 1979), 319-356; S. Coren and J. S. Girgus, *Seeing Is Deceiving: The Psychology of Visual Illusions* (Hillsdale, NJ: Lawrence Erlbaum Associates, 1978).

6. C. G. Gross, et al., "Inferior temporal cortex as a visual integration area," in *Cortical Integration* ed. F. Reinoso-Suárez and C. Ajmone-Marsan (New York: Raven Press, 1984), 291-315.

7. I. Rock, *Orientation and Form* (New York: Academic Press, 1973); I. Rock, *Perception* (New York: Scientific American Library, 1984).

8. S. Carey, "The development of face recognition," in *Perceiving and Remembering Faces*, ed. G. Davies, H. Ellis, & J. Shepherd (New York: Academic Press, 1981).

9. R. N. Shepard, "Ecological constraints on internal representation: Resonant kinematics of perceiving, imagining, thinking, and dreaming," *Psychological Review* 91 (1984): 417-447.

10. R. N. Shepard, "The role of transformations in spatial cognition," in *Spatial Cognition: Brain Bases and Development*, ed. J. Stiles-Davis, M. Kritchevsky, and U. Bellugi (Hillsdale, NJ: Lawrence Erlbaum Associates, 1988), 81-110.

11. For a discussion of a number of similar subjective phenomena of lightness contrast, see Chapter 10 of the book by G. Kanizsa, *Organization in Vision: Essays on Gestalt Perception* (New York: Praeger, 1979); pages 170-180.

12. L. S. Penrose and R. Penrose, "Impossible objects: A special type of visual illusion," *British Journal of Psychology* 49 (1958): 31-33.

13. *The graphic work of* M. C. *Escher* (New York: Duell, Sloan and Pearce, 1960). See the lithograph, *Ascending and Descending*, on page 35.

14. R. N. Shepard, "Demonstrations of circular components of pitch," *Journal of the Audio Engineering Society* 31 (1983): 641-649. (Earlier versions of the illustration were used in the article and the film listed in Note 11 for Part I.)

15. H. Klüver, *Mescal and the Mechanisms of Hallucination* (Chicago: University of Chicago Press, 1966); R. N. Shepard, "Externalization of mental images and the act of creation," in *Visual Learning, Thinking, and Communication*, ed. B. S. Randhawa and W. E. Coffman (New York: Academic Press, 1978), 133-189.

16. H.-O. Peitgen and P. H. Richter, *The Beauty of Fractals* (Berlin: Springer-Verlag, 1986).

17. M. H. Pirenne, *Optics, Painting, and Photography* (Cambridge: Cambridge University Press, 1970); photographs of the Pozzo ceiling are shown on pages 79ff.

18. Ibid.

19. M. Kubovy, *The Psychology of Perspective and Renaissance Art* (Cambridge: Cambridge University Press, 1986).

20. G. P. Sackett, "Monkeys reared in isolation with pictures as visual input: Evidence for an innnate releasing mechanism," *Science*, 154 (1966): 1468-1473.

21. H. Sedgwick, "The geometry of spatial layout in pictorial representation," in *The Perception of Pictures*, ed. M. Hagen (New York: Academic Press, 1980), vol. 1.

22. M. Kubovy, *The Psychology of Perspective and Renaissance Art*, 77.

23. H. von Helmholtz, *Treatise on Physiological Optics*, 3rd German ed., 3 vols., trans. P. P. C. Southall (New York: Dover, 1962), vol. 3.

24. W. H. Ittleson, *The Ames Demonstrations in Perception* (Princeton, NJ: Princeton University Press, 1952).

25. R. N. Shepard, "Evolution of a mesh between principles of the mind and regularities of the world," in *The Latest on the Best: Essays on Evolution and Optimality*, ed. J. Dupré (Cambridge, MA: MIT Press/Bradford Books, 1987), 251-275; R. N. Shepard, "Ecological constraints on internal representation."

26. R. N. Shepard, "Internal representation of universal regularities: A challenge for connectionism," in *Neural Connections, Mental Computation*, ed. L. Nadel, et al. (Cambridge, MA: MIT Press/Bradford Books, 1989), 104-134.

27. D. N. Perkins, *Geometry and the Perception of Pictures: Three Studies*, Project Zero, Technical Report no. 5 (Cambridge, MA: Harvard University, 1971); D. N. Perkins, "Visual discrimination between rectangular and nonrectangular parallelepipeds," *Perception & Psychophysics* 12 (1972): 396-400; R. N. Shepard, "Psychophysical complementarity" in *Perceptual organization*, ed. M. Kubovy and J. Pomerantz (Hillsdale, NJ: Lawrence Erlbaum Associates, 1981), 279-341. (Figure III-16 is adapted from Figures 10.6 and 10.7 on pages 304 and 306 of this last article.)

28. J.-P. Sartre, *Nausea*, trans. R. Baldick (Harmondsworth, U. K.: Penguin Books, 1965).

29. E. Gombrich, *Art and Illusion: A Study in the Psychology of Pictorial Representation* (Princeton, NJ: Princeton University Press, 1960).

30. R. N. Shepard, "Psychomusicology forum: Roger Shepard responds," *Psychomusicology* 3 (1984): 57-59; R. N. Shepard, "Ecological constraints on internal representation."

31. J. J. Gibson, *The Senses Considered as Perceptual Systems*; J. J. Gibson, *The Ecological Approach to Visual Perception*.

32. M. H. Pirenne, *Optics, Painting, and Photography*, 99-100.

33. Ibid., 86-87.

34. Ibid., 98.

35. M. Kubovy, *The Psychology of Perspective and Renaissance Art*, 137-149.

36. W. Köhler, *The Place of Value in a World of Facts* (New York: Liveright, 1938).

37. A. Yonas, "Infants' responses to optical information for collision," in *Development of Perception: Psychobiological Perspectives. Vol. 2: The Visual System*, ed. R. N. Aslin, J. R. Alberts, and M. R. Peterson (New York: Academic Press, 1981).

38. See, for example, B. Mundkur, *The Cult of the Serpent: An Inter-disciplinary Survey of Its Manifestations and Origins* (Albany, NY: State University of New York Press, 1983), 219; and, for other evidence of innate reactions to visual stimuli, see G. P. Sackett, "Monkeys reared in isolation with pictures as visual input: Evidence for an innnate releasing mechanism" (Note 20).

39. Behavioral evidence has been reported by D. K. Candland, S. Briggs, and J. Hallal, "Assessing nonhuman primate categories of perception" (Paper presented at the twenty-sixth annual meeting of the Psychonomic Society, Boston, Nov. 22, 1985);

R. C. Kyes and D. K. Candland, "Baboon (*Papio hamadryas*) visual preferences for socially relevant stimuli" (Paper presented at the twenty-fourth annual meeting of the Psychonomic Society, San Diego, Nov. 18, 1983); and neurophysiological evidence has been reported by C. G. Gross, et al., "Inferior temporal cortex as a visual integration area" (Note 6).

40. R. Fantz, "The origin of form perception," *Scientific American* 204 (1961): 66-72; J. Kagan, "The distribution of attention in infancy," *Perception and Its Disorders*, The Association for Reserach in Nervous and Mental Disease, 48 (1970): 214-237.

41. R. N. Shepard, "Toward a universal law of generalization for psychological science," *Science 37* (1987): 1317-1323.

42. R. N. Shepard, "Ecological constraints on internal representation."

43. Variants of the idea that shape can be specified in terms of degrees of self-similarity under different transformations are proposed in R. N. Shepard, "Psychophysical complementarity;" R. N. Shepard, "The role of transformations in spatial cognition," in *Spatial cognition: Brain bases and development.*

44. H. Klüver, *Mescal and the Mechanisms of Hallucination* (Chicago: University of Chicago Press, 1966)

45. R. N. Shepard, "Externalization of mental images and the act of creation," in *Visual Learning, Thinking, and Communication*, ed. B. S. Randhawa and W. E. Coffman (New York: Academic Press, 1978), 133-189. (The color plates appear between pages 176 and 177.)

46. Ibid., 173-174.

47. Sir J. F. W. Herschel, *Familiar Lectures on Scientific Subjects* (London: Strahan, 1867); see Herschel's lecture, "On sensorial vision."

48. R. N. Shepard, "Externalization of mental images;" J. R. Newman, "James Clerk Maxwell," *Scientific American* 192 (1955): 58-71.

49. R. N. Shepard, "The kaleidosopic brain," *Psychology Today* June (1983): 62-68; R. N. Shepard, C. Downing, and T. Putnam, "Inner visions," *Psychology Today* February (1985): 66-69.

50. B. B. Mandelbrot, *The Fractal Geometry of Nature* (New York: W. H. Freeman, 1982).

51. Quoted in G. E. Moore, *Principia Ethica* (Cambridge: Cambridge University Press, 1968), 206.